the raw deal cookbook

the
raw deal
cookbook

Over 100 Truly Simple
Plant-Based Recipes
for the Real World

Emily Monaco

SONOMA
PRESS

contents

INTRODUCTION

I've been eating a plant-based diet for decades, but no matter how much I love my vegetables, the jump from plant-based to raw seemed a little extreme at first, even to me.

It was easy to go from omnivore to mostly vegetarian. It all started in a boarding school cafeteria, where the meat options left much to be desired, and an enormous salad bar was the focal point of the room. I'd read work by Michael Pollan on the subject, so it just made sense to cut out meat entirely.

As I got older and started cooking in my own kitchen, I became what is now known as a "flexitarian." I was happy to eat meat when other people were making it—especially sustainably raised, grass-fed meats—but generally, I found it not worth the trouble to make animal protein a regular staple of my own kitchen. Not only did I find vegetables to be more delicious and fun to prepare, but I also appreciated their abundance of health benefits.

While I understood the benefits of going all in with a raw food diet, the cons always seemed to outweigh the pros. For instance, there'd be no more big batches of chili to make on the weekends and help me save time during the week. And what about all the equipment I'd need to transform my kitchen into a raw food prep station? Plus, even though I loved my plant-based recipes, I couldn't see how I was ever going to be satisfied eating salad for breakfast, lunch, and dinner.

Luckily, the cons I had in my mind were founded on misconceptions. First of all, even the most hardcore raw foodies today say that an entirely raw food diet can be unrealistic and, worse, unhealthy; eating raw foods about 75 percent of the time is just fine and allows you to take advantage of essential nutrients like vitamin B_{12}, vitamin D, and omega-3 fatty acids, which are hard to get from a fully raw, plant-based diet. You can easily integrate one, two, or three raw food recipes into your daily or weekly meals, and many of these recipes can be easily doubled, allowing you to plan ahead and stock up on leftovers.

As for bulky and expensive gadgets? I didn't buy anything new for my kitchen, and I was still able to tackle a whole host of raw food recipes. While you can always invest in a gadget if you feel that it will help you prepare meals more quickly, all the recipes in this book can be made with tools that you'll find in any well-stocked kitchen.

When I started to incorporate raw foods into my diet, I found that they were actually more filling than cooked foods, but it's definitely a different kind of full. The high-fiber fruits and vegetables that make up the majority of a raw food diet just don't allow for the same level of satiety that you get from meals made on the stove or in the oven. This means that it can take a while to get used to the new kind of full, but once you do, you will realize all the other benefits a raw food diet can have on your pace of life. There's no more sluggishness or sleepiness after a meal, no more need to rest or nap after eating. After a meal, I feel invigorated and ready to go, and I find that when I eat a balanced raw meal, digestion is easier and much more comfortable. As a result, I also find that I sleep better—I never feel drowsy during the day, and I don't fall asleep in front of the television every evening anymore. I sleep soundly and wake up refreshed and ready to go!

My intention with this book is to offer an easy way to approach raw cooking, whether it's for a few lunches here and there, a couple of meals throughout the week or month, or an entire lifestyle change. Whatever your

approach, you'll soon see just how easy and fulfilling raw food meals are to make and how flavorful and satiating they can be.

Many raw food recipes call for long lists of hard-to-find ingredients, but that's not what you'll find in this book. Here, I've compiled a trove of dishes that are based on fresh produce, herbs, spices, and other foods that are stocked in most big-chain supermarkets. I do, however, encourage you to buy local and organic produce whenever you can, to be sure that you're getting only the most healthy fruits and vegetables. This is important for everyone, but it's especially essential when you're eating raw. Before you jump onto the raw food bandwagon, spend some time reading through part 1 of this book. There, I've outlined the essentials of a raw food diet, assembled helpful tips and tricks for fitting it into your lifestyle, and included several weeks' worth of meal plans to help you get used to "cooking" raw.

As for the recipes themselves, they're far from just salads. In part 2, you'll find more than 100 raw food meals, drinks, snacks, and yes, even desserts that are as varied and full of flavor as they are brimming with nutrients and essential enzymes.

So, what are you waiting for? Let's get raw, shall we?

going raw

raw PART ONE

CHAPTER 1

raw food
for the
real world

When I first heard about raw diets, I was definitely intrigued. There was no denying the vibrant flavor of fresh fruits and vegetables, and I had eaten enough raw meals to know that they fill me up just as much as cooked meals do, without ever leaving me overly stuffed. But to go from there to completely overhauling my diet, buying all sorts of equipment, and possibly never eating some of my favorite cooked foods again? I just never felt ready to make the leap.

I decided instead to read up on the subject, and what I learned immediately debunked my fears. For instance, most experts don't recommend that you eat raw foods for every meal, every day, since a 100 percent raw diet lacks some nutrients that your body needs to thrive. And perhaps the clincher: Raw food recipes do not require specialized tools and gadgets—everything I needed was already in my tiny kitchen. In the pages that follow, I'll walk you through the principles, logistics, and health benefits of the raw food lifestyle, and give you all the tips and tricks you need to make it a part of your real-world routine.

what is raw?

Many people who start eating a raw diet make the leap from a vegetarian or vegan diet. Whereas a vegetarian avoids only meat and fish, a vegan diet excludes all animal products, including milk and derivatives like cheese, butter, and yogurt, plus eggs and, in some cases, even honey.

A raw food diet is similar to a vegan diet, with a few added restrictions. In a raw food diet, food cannot be heated above 118°F. This means that while some foods can be dried in a very low oven or dehydrator, for example, most foods are consumed in their natural state. The reason for this is to conserve as many as possible of the essential enzymes and vitamins that are contained in raw ingredients. That might seem fairly limited, but as you'll soon learn, there are loads of things that you can do with raw foods to make them delicious!

THE BUILDING BLOCKS

A raw food diet is made up of raw fruits, vegetables, nuts, and some grains. Because certain grains, such as wheat, cannot be consumed raw, they are excluded from a raw food diet. Other foods, such as legumes and beans, need to be sprouted before they can be consumed.

These foods can be prepared in a variety of ways to bring out their flavors and different textures. It is common, for example, to marinate raw vegetables and fruits to make them even more flavorful and break down some of the harder-to-digest elements that they contain. And, of course, there are smoothies—it's much easier to ingest the variety of fruits and vegetables you need if you whir them through the blender and drink them instead of eating them.

You'll also find that many nuts and seeds can be blended or puréed to make creamy sauces and dips. In fact, much of the fun in making raw food recipes is seeing how you can transform familiar ingredients into new and exciting foods: cauliflower rice, raw tomato sauce, zucchini noodles . . . all will become regular parts of your diet as you explore the variety that raw foods can offer.

FOODS TO ENJOY

Raw vegetables

Sea vegetables

Raw fruits

Dried fruits

Sprouted grains

Sprouted legumes

Raw nuts and seeds

Fermented foods

BALANCE

As with any way of eating, a fulfilling raw food diet requires balance. The key to getting the most fulfillment out of a raw food diet is to vary the ingredients you use and the way that they are prepared as much as possible.

When approaching raw food, be sure to consider balance, both in each meal and in your day as a whole. Most balance problems can be avoided just by making sure you're eating enough food. When you exclude more calorie-dense foods like dairy and meat from your diet, you need to compensate with other calorie-dense foods; in raw diets, this is usually nuts, seeds, and avocados. Just be sure that you're including a blend of fruits, vegetables, and nuts or seeds at every meal so that you stay satiated and maintain a varied and complete intake of vitamins and minerals. If you're always eating the same thing, you may miss out on some key nutritional elements. That's why starting your morning with a smoothie or fresh-pressed juice is so important: You can vary the ingredients each day with a cocktail of different vitamins and minerals, as well as healthy fiber in the case of the smoothie.

Balance should also appear on your plate. The best way I've found to build a healthy raw food meal is to start with a central vegetable and work out from there, creating dressings and seasonings with fattier nuts, seeds, and avocados, and consuming fruit in juices, with breakfast, or in desserts. Feel free to let your eye be your guide: Including lots of different colors on your plate will not only make your food appear more appetizing, but it will also ensure that you've got a mix of different vitamins and minerals in each dish, keeping your diet as balanced as possible.

THE RAW FOOD PYRAMID

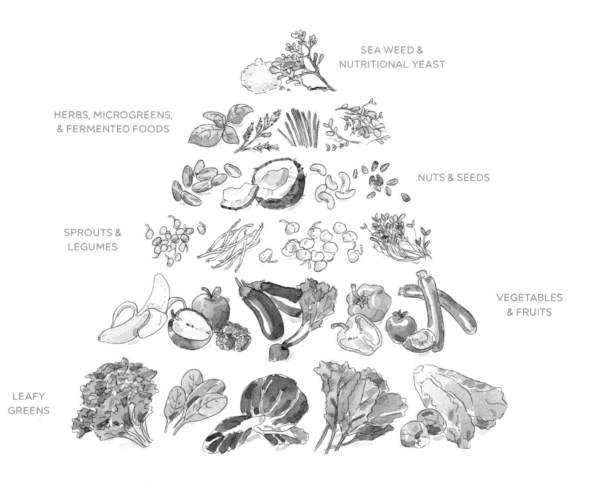

SEA WEED &
NUTRITIONAL YEAST

HERBS, MICROGREENS,
& FERMENTED FOODS

NUTS & SEEDS

SPROUTS &
LEGUMES

VEGETABLES
& FRUITS

LEAFY
GREENS

This raw adaption of a traditional food pyramid
outlines the components of a balanced raw diet.

It's important not to dive into raw food blindly, and especially not all at once. Even if you've already been eating sensibly, raw food is definitely an adjustment, and trying to jump straight in without any guidance is a recipe for failure.

In this book, I'll show you how to go raw gradually over the course of one month. During the first week, you'll eat raw breakfasts and lunches but cooked dinners. During week two, you'll swap out three of your cooked dinners for raw ones. In week three, you'll eat 100 percent raw foods for seven full days, and in week four, it'll be up to you to reintroduce a few cooked meals, depending on what feels right to you.

But just because you're not eating raw all the time doesn't mean that cooked meals should be considered "cheat" meals! This mentality is like taking one step forward and two steps back. Instead, base your cooked meals predominantly on whole foods and plants for the best nutritional value. For instance, you might want to include a piece of steamed fish for the omega-3 fatty acids, or add a bit of cooked tomato to a dish for the increased lycopene. This flexible approach is all about finding balance and discovering how you can make a raw food diet work for you and your daily life.

the health benefits

The main idea behind the raw food diet is that cooking removes many of the essential enzymes and phytonutrients contained in raw fruits and vegetables. It makes sense, then, to take full advantage of consuming these foods raw, to absorb as many of these essential elements as possible.

But what are enzymes and phytonutrients, and why are they so important?

Enzymes are the body's helpers; they facilitate different jobs that need to be carried out by the body, including digestion. Enzymes are naturally present in the body, but by consuming raw enzymes, the body's natural enzymes can be used for other things; the ones in your food help you digest and metabolize, so the ones naturally present in your body can complete other tasks. This means that you don't get sluggish and lethargic after eating, but rather feel rejuvenated and energized.

Phytonutrients are trace elements that help support vitamins and minerals by ensuring that your cells function properly and strengthen the immune system. Unlike vitamins and minerals, phytonutrients aren't

100% RAW?

Some raw food dieters claim that the best way to go raw is to kick all cooked foods out of your life completely, but many experts in the field now say that's not really ideal. Some of the biggest names in raw food, like Victoria Boutenko, Elaina Love, and Chad Sarno, are including steamed and even lightly cooked versions of some foods in their diets, saying that this is the optimal way to get the most nutritional value from their meals.

There are multiple reasons for including some cooked foods in a mostly raw lifestyle. The advantages of certain foods are accentuated or changed by cooking— for instance, tomatoes boast increased phytochemicals when cooked, but a better vitamin C content when raw. In fact, many anti-carcinogenic phytochemicals and carotenoids are better absorbed by the body when they are in their cooked rather than raw forms, meaning that cooked carrots and winter squash are good to include in your diet as well.

In some cases, eating raw foods can even be counterproductive: Cooking tough-to-digest vegetables will make them easier to digest, and will allow your body to conserve enzymes for other uses. If you're following a mostly raw diet plan, any cooking should be done via steaming or boiling, which do not form the same heat-related toxins that dry cooking techniques do.

This isn't to say that you should be cooking everything. Between 10 and 20 percent of vitamins and minerals are lost during the cooking process of whole foods. The key is in finding the correct percentage of raw foods to include in your regular meals—a 60 to 80 percent raw diet is best to maintain the health benefits and still supply your body with the essential nutrients it needs.

Feel free to vary your intake of raw food from week to week, depending on your mood and how comfortable you are with the diet. Increasing your raw food consumption even a little bit will allow you to take advantage of many of the benefits, though most people say that consuming less than 50 percent raw food means that these benefits are difficult to notice in day-to-day life.

essential for survival, which is likely why you haven't heard much about them in the past, at least not as a group. You may have heard of some individual phytonutrients, including carotenoids, which can be converted into vitamin A by the body; lycopene, which has been linked to lowered cancer risks; and lutein, which helps protect the eyes from age-related degeneration.

Both of these elements are essential to better health, yet when cooked, they are often destroyed. By following a raw food diet—or simply including more raw foods in your regular routine—your body will get a noticeable boost from the extra enzymes and phytonutrients you consume.

In addition to the absorption of these two elements—and in many cases, because of it—there are many other benefits to going raw. Here are just a few of my favorites:

YOU'LL HAVE MORE ENERGY. Creating the enzymes needed to digest food takes time and energy. When the enzymes in raw food can take care of digestion themselves, your body doesn't need to create them, and you're left with much more energy for other things.

YOU'LL HAVE BETTER DIGESTION. While your digestion may slow down and sort of . . . stop things up at the beginning of your raw food diet, eventually you'll notice that your digestion will improve overall, particularly if you're getting a good balance of fermented foods and healthy fats along with your raw veggies. Making sure that you chew properly and consume good sources of both soluble and insoluble fiber are also important for proper digestion.

YOU'LL LOSE WEIGHT. Because raw foods tend to be low in calories, many people find themselves operating at a calorie deficit while on a raw food diet, even when they eat until they are completely full.

YOUR SKIN AND HAIR WILL BE HEALTHIER. Some of the minerals that benefit skin and hair health are present in raw foods like leafy greens, raw almonds, orange root vegetables, and raw pumpkin seeds. You'll also notice that by removing animal fats from your diet, any blemishes will soon clear up, and your skin will look better than it has in years.

YOUR RISK OF HEART DISEASE WILL DECREASE. There are two sides to this health benefit. The first is the belief that the enzymes in raw food and the alkalinity of the diet in general make you healthier and more resistant to disease. But even though the science is still out on this particular claim, upping your intake of fruits and vegetables and decreasing your intake of saturated fats is a great way to decrease your risk of heart disease, no matter who you ask.

YOU'LL SLEEP BETTER. Studies have shown that people who switch to a raw food diet need less sleep, and sleep generally better than those who do not eat as many raw foods. Esme Stevens, founder of Raw Food Europe, maintains that proponents of a raw food diet need up to three hours less sleep per night than people eating a traditional diet. This is due to the fact that insulin is better regulated on a raw food diet, so you don't suffer from exhausting and taxing sugar spikes and crashes. Furthermore, the increased alkalinity of the body on a raw food diet encourages better sleep, with fewer disruptions.

raw food and you

By now, you're likely starting to wonder what all this information means for you. The answer is complicated, because there's no one solution for everybody—it's up to you to decide what works and what doesn't. That being said, however, eating a couple of salads during the week doesn't count as "going raw." If you want to see real results, you'll have to make a real commitment. As a baseline, strive for a regular routine of raw breakfasts and lunches and the occasional raw dinner. Then tweak your personalized plan here and there, depending on how your body feels.

In this book, you'll find tons of recipes that work for busy people with modern lives. But above all, this book will be your guide to approaching raw food with your life, your desires, and your everyday patterns in mind.

MAKE IT A LIFESTYLE

Raw food is more than a diet; it's a lifestyle. In order to make raw food work for you, you're going to need to make other changes to your daily life as well. Your entire lifestyle should be healthier, not just the way you eat.

Raw foods should be incorporated into your life as part of a multifaceted plan to get healthier, along with exercise, adequate sleep, and stress management. All these elements play a part in making sure that your new lifestyle sticks and does what it's supposed to do.

As with your slow but steady approach to raw food, these other elements of your new lifestyle can be integrated gradually. Consider getting active three times a week, even if it's just for a brisk 30-minute walk. Enjoy some destressing time at a moment that works for you: in the morning with your raw smoothie or in the evening with a relaxing herbal

COMMON PITFALLS

Ready to start your new raw food regime? Hold your horses. It's important to be aware of the unhealthy patterns you could slip into when making the transition to raw.

TOO MUCH SUGAR. One common mistake that newbies find themselves making is overeating fruit or some of the natural sugars that are allowed on a raw food diet, such as coconut sugar or raw honey. After all, most of us have a bit of a sweet tooth, and it's much easier to gorge on berries than it is to gorge on cauliflower! Remember that sweet foods should always be eaten in moderation, and if all else fails, follow your gut. If you find yourself frequently bloated, suffering from diarrhea, or dealing with severe sugar cravings, you might be eating too much fruit.

OVERLOADING ON FATTY FOODS. Avocados, nuts, seeds, and other fatty raw foods make us feel fuller and more satisfied, so it can be easy to eat them in excess. You may even find that you don't recognize what fullness actually feels like when you're eating raw food at first because you won't get that heavy, overly stuffed sensation at the end of a meal. Fattier foods do tend to give you that feeling, but they should never be your main source of sustenance on a raw diet.

NOT ENOUGH PROTEIN. One big worry for new raw foodies is where their protein is coming from. The good news is that it's easy to consume the right amount of protein on a raw food diet if you plan well. The recommended dietary allowance (RDA) is 0.8 grams of protein per kilogram of body weight, meaning that a 115-pound woman should be consuming 41.6 grams daily. If you have a salad for lunch made with 2 cups of kale, 1 ounce of cashews, and ½ cup of sprouted lentils, you've already eaten 16.5 grams of protein—more than one-third of your recommended daily intake.

Most of these pitfalls can be solved via trial and error. Are you making vegetables the bulk of your plate? Are you feeling full? Are you listening to your body's signals? Are you eating a variety of foods and colors? If the answers to these questions are yes, you're well on your way.

infusion and a book. Having some downtime, particularly away from noise and screens, allows you to take stock of your day and consider the challenges and events ahead.

If you include raw food as one part of a whole lifestyle change, you'll see the benefits even more rapidly, and you'll also find that one part of your lifestyle leads into another: Eating raw will give you more energy for activity, and engaging in daily activity will help you sleep better and become more relaxed. And when you're more relaxed, you can enjoy your daily activities to the fullest.

10 TIPS FOR A RAW FOOD LIFESTYLE

1. **PLAN AHEAD.** The key to success on a raw food diet is planning ahead. You might balk at first at how often you're going to the grocery store or the fact that you're spending a lot more time in the kitchen. Try blocking off a few hours on Sunday—or any other day when you have time—to plan out all your meals for the week, prep anything you can in advance, and make a shopping list for the week ahead. You may decide to shop only once a week, or maybe you'll do one big run on the weekend and pick up little things every day as needed. Find a plan that works for you, and give yourself the tools and the time you need to succeed.

2. **MAKE IT FUN.** Raw food recipes are easy to prepare, but they often involve time-consuming steps like chopping, grating, and marinating. Lighten the load—and your mood—by inviting family and friends to help out in the kitchen. Not only will this give you some moral support as you test out your new raw lifestyle, but it will also encourage you to enjoy the process and explore all the different flavors, textures, and preparations that are possible with raw ingredients. More importantly, when prep time is also social time, it becomes something you look forward to all week.

3. **DON'T THINK OF IT AS A LIMITATION.** One of the first things you might be tempted to say when you start a raw food diet is, "I can't eat that." But don't let raw food limit you—instead, think of all the things you're gaining with this choice. By planning some healthy snacks in advance, particularly things you can carry with you, like raw whole fruits, crudités, and On-the-Go Energy Bites (page 166), you won't be tempted to say, "I can't."

4. **GET YOUR FRIENDS AND FAMILY INVOLVED.** If the people close to you don't understand this lifestyle change, they may feel like the enemy, constantly offering you bites of tempting things you're trying to avoid. So educate them! Explain why you decided to go raw, and share one of your favorite recipes with them. At the very least, they'll become more educated and understand your choice—and if you're lucky, they might even decide to join in the fun and become your new raw buddy.

5. **TAKE BABY STEPS.** Don't feel as though you need to make every change at once. If you're just starting to eat raw food and have always hated cauliflower, then don't make a cauliflower rice dish for your first meal. Start with foods you love, then work your way toward new

discoveries. Trying to make too many changes at once is just asking for trouble; getting comfortable with small changes and building from there will be the key to your success.

6. DISCOVER NEW FOODS. A raw diet can feel limiting, but there are so many exciting foods to try and discover. Try to set a goal of preparing a new food once every week or two. From kelp noodles to goji berries to cacao nibs, you'll soon discover a host of exciting flavors—and maybe even find some new favorites.

7. DON'T BEAT YOURSELF UP. You forgot to pack your raw lunch and skipped out to Subway at noon. The kale you were saving for today went off, so you made scrambled eggs instead. You might stumble on the road to raw food nirvana, and that's okay. The most important thing is to not look at these moments as failures, but as steps along the way. Pick yourself up, and get back in the game.

8. CHEW. One of the most important things you'll learn when eating a raw food diet is the importance of chewing. So many of the foods we're used to eating don't actually require that much mastication, but the insoluble fibers in common raw foods like crucifers need to be chewed—a lot—in order for the body to properly digest them. Chewing your food thoroughly has several benefits: It means that you eat more slowly, so you notice more quickly when you're full, and it also helps you digest more efficiently and effectively, allowing your body to absorb all the vitamins and minerals in your food. Your digestive tract will thank you, too.

9. KEEP A JOURNAL. The beginning of a new food regime is always exciting, but once it becomes a part of your regular routine, you might stop noticing the benefits, at least in your day-to-day life. Keep a journal of how you're feeling each day, and when you get discouraged, look back at what you've written. Has your sleep improved? Your mood? Your skin? Looking back at past accomplishments will help you continue to forge forward.

10. ENJOY IT. Raw food has its limitations, but above all, it's fun. Pick delicious recipes, get to know your local farmers, and educate yourself and your family about different kinds of food. Make raw food work for you and your lifestyle, and you'll soon wonder why you didn't make the change ages ago.

faqs

WHAT'S THE BEST SOURCE OF PROTEIN ON A RAW FOOD DIET? Leafy greens are a good source of protein, but you need to eat a lot of them—2 cups of kale has about 4 grams of protein. Other good sources are nuts, seeds, and sprouted legumes: 1 cup of sprouted lentils has 17 grams of protein. What you might not realize is that nearly every fruit contains some protein, too, and with the amount of fruit you'll be consuming in your smoothies and desserts, you'll reach your quota in no time. Try tracking your protein intake for the first two weeks—you'll see how quickly things add up.

AM I GOING TO BE MISSING OUT ON ANY IMPORTANT VITAMINS AND MINERALS? There are only a few vitamins and minerals you won't be getting enough of on a raw food diet. One is vitamin B_{12}, which is found only in animal products. A vitamin B_{12} deficiency takes a long time to develop, but it can be very serious and may result in anemia. Many raw vegans take B_{12} supplements, and some brands of nutritional yeast add B_{12} to their product as well, which can make it a great additional source. Do bear in mind, though, that the amount of nutritional yeast that is usually used in recipes is not enough to meet your RDA for vitamin B_{12}.

You may also need to find alternative sources of vitamin D and omega-3 fatty acids, as neither of these nutrients are easily absorbed by the human body from plant sources. Both of these can be added to the diet via supplements. You should also keep track of how much selenium, zinc, and iron you are getting to make sure you're meeting the RDA of these minerals; all are present in plant sources, but it's common for new raw foodies to develop deficiencies of these minerals if they don't pay attention to their intakes.

ARE THERE ANY DOWNSIDES TO EATING A RAW FOOD DIET? Sure, just as there are downsides to anything. You definitely have to plan more and be more organized, and you'll need to be on top of managing your menu so that you don't have dietary deficiencies. Some people can also suffer digestive discomfort, and others operate at a severe calorie deficit, which isn't healthy either. As long as you plan ahead and keep track of what you're eating, especially at the beginning, you should be able to overcome any downsides easily.

IS EATING RAW MORE EXPENSIVE THAN EATING COOKED FOOD? Not necessarily. Some raw food ingredients, like hemp seeds, chia seeds, and flax seeds, are expensive, but for the most part, you'll just be buying organic fruits and veggies, which are much cheaper than meat. The one thing you'll notice is that you may have to shop more frequently, as you'll be relying on foods that have a short shelf life rather than canned and jarred foods that can be kept in the pantry. But if you compare your overall monthly grocery bill, you'll likely see that it's about the same or even a bit lower when you switch to raw foods.

CAN I SAVE MY LEFTOVERS AND EAT THEM THE NEXT DAY? That depends on whom you ask. Some people say that minerals and vitamins start to leach out of raw foods the longer you keep them—which is why the raw food diet is known as the "living" food diet in some circles—and certain dishes need to be eaten right away or you risk the vegetables in them releasing too much water and not being as appetizing. However, if you plan ahead, you should be able to make enough of certain dishes for leftovers and to keep other foods—for example, the pulp that remains from making almond milk—to use in other dishes. And there are some raw dishes, like fermented foods and chia puddings, that actually get better with age. One of the keys to planning ahead won't necessarily be making enough for leftovers, but rather preparing your ingredients in advance so that the dish can be assembled quickly and easily.

ARE THERE ANY FOODS I SHOULD AVOID EATING RAW? There are foods that you absolutely cannot digest raw, including cassava, potatoes, and certain mushrooms. Some foods are easier to digest when they've been marinated or soaked, including certain nuts and grains, beans and lentils, mushrooms, and crucifers. The recipes in this book will guide you toward making these foods palatable.

IS RAW FOOD SAFE TO FEED TO MY KIDS? Yes, of course! The question, however, is whether a growing child's body can be sustained on raw food alone. Many doctors believe that a child's developing digestive system may not be able to pull the nutrients out of raw foods as effectively as an adult's, so you might want to opt for closer to a 50/50 ratio of raw to cooked food for children. Always consult with your pediatrician before you make any drastic changes to your child's diet.

A SPOTLIGHT ON FERMENTED FOODS

Many assume that because there's no cooking in raw food, there's not much transformation of ingredients, but that's just not true. Fermented foods are a key element of raw food diets, as they improve your general gut health. They're also a great idea for busy raw food proponents, as they can be prepared in advance and enjoyed later, when you don't have much time to "cook."

The idea behind the fermenting of a food is to encourage the production of natural, healthy bacteria. These bacteria feed on the sugar and starch in the original food, creating lactic acid. This not only preserves the food, but it also creates B vitamins and omega-3 fatty acids that are generally lacking in raw food diets.

Consuming fermented foods improves your digestion and preserves important enzymes in what you eat. It also boosts your immune function and can balance blood sugar. And as if that isn't enough, fermented foods also add unique flavors, thanks to the production of the souring lactic acid. Some common fermented foods include sauerkraut and kimchi, which can be eaten either on their own or as part of another recipe.

Natural fermentation is easy to start at home—all you need is a large jar that you can keep on the counter, with an airtight lid to keep out oxygen. While some people purchase fancy fermenters, you can also

make your own with a simple mason jar: Just pour a half-inch layer of olive oil on top of the ferment to make sure you have an airtight seal.

Don't be worried about leaving food out on the counter, as the controlled environment of fermentation kills off any bad bacteria, leaving behind only the beneficial probiotics that make the consumption of fermented foods such a great idea. If you see any white sludge, mold, slime, or brown or pink portions of the food, or if you smell a yeasty odor instead of an acidic odor when you open your jar, it has likely been contaminated with bad bacteria, and you should throw it away, wash the jar, and start again. See chapter 10 for some basic fermentation recipes to get you started.

CHAPTER 2

the raw kitchen

The first step in starting a raw food diet is to get your kitchen ready. After all, you wouldn't start any big project without first obtaining the appropriate tools, would you?

Don't worry, though, we're not talking about expensive or hard-to-find gadgets. It's more about stocking your pantry and refrigerator with useful ingredients that will keep you on track and make for a seamless transition to eating raw.

10 transformative ingredients

Of course, there's a whole world of fruits and vegetables for you to explore, but as you start cooking raw, you'll notice that certain ingredients form the base for many of your meals. Here are 10 raw foods that you'll be reaching for again and again:

AVOCADO. Creamy and mild, avocado will feature in many recipes, both sweet and savory. This fruit is full of healthy fats and has a lot of staying power, keeping you fuller longer. It's a preferred snack for many raw foodies, as it's delicious and satiating.

CACAO NIBS. Thought that a raw food diet would mean giving up chocolate? Think again! Raw cacao nibs offer chocolate flavor and nutrients to a variety of raw desserts.

CASHEWS. Many raw ingredients are crunchy, but raw cashews, when soaked in water, can be puréed into something smooth and creamy, which is why they're the base for many sauces. Cashews do go rancid quickly, however, so you'll want to buy them in small amounts and restock regularly.

CAULIFLOWER. Relatively mild in flavor, raw cauliflower is the key to creating raw substitutes for rice and couscous. Regardless of your past relationship, it's going to be your new best friend.

CHIA SEEDS. You may have already discovered the wonder of chia seeds. These little protein-packed seeds expand when soaked in liquid to create a gel that thickens puddings, juices, and smoothies without cooking.

DATES. Because of their natural sweetness, dates are often used as a sugar replacement in raw diets. Their sticky texture also helps hold desserts like cookies and truffles together.

KALE. This dark leafy green has had its day in the sun, but while the trend may have passed, kale's impressive roster of nutritional benefits has not. Kale can be blitzed into green smoothies or massaged with vinaigrette to form the base for a filling, raw salad.

NUTRITIONAL YEAST. Not only does nutritional yeast contain high amounts of vitamin B_{12}, but it's also got an umami flavor that makes it the secret to "cheese" sauces in raw food recipes.

SPROUTED LENTILS. These little legumes are an important vegan source of protein, and when sprouted, they're totally safe to eat raw. They'll provide a lot of bulk for your meals.

ZUCCHINI. When shredded into long, thin ribbons (or "zoodles"), zucchini becomes a delicious raw alternative to pasta, topped with a variety of sauces.

stocking your pantry

Stocking the pantry for your raw food adventure may seem intimidating at first, especially given that many of your new staples—like adzuki beans and hemp hearts—might be things you've never tried before. But soon you'll find that having a few basic ingredients on hand will make raw food recipes a breeze to prepare. In addition to the following pantry items, you should also make sure your refrigerator is stocked with fresh, in-season produce at all times. As a rule, try to choose organic whenever possible, but to save yourself some money, check out the Clean Fifteen list on page 219 to learn which fruits and vegetables are safe when conventionally grown.

Your raw foods pantry should always include the following items:

- **Raw nuts and seeds:** almonds, cacao nibs, cashews, chia seeds, flax seeds, hemp hearts, macadamia nuts, pumpkin seeds, sunflower seeds

- **Fresh herbs:** basil, chives, cilantro, parsley

- **Sprouting legumes:** adzuki beans, chickpeas, lentils

- **Sweeteners:** agave nectar, coconut sugar, dates, raw honey

- **Spices and flavorings:** chili powder, fresh garlic, fresh ginger, nutritional yeast, pink Himalayan salt, raw tahini

- **Liquid flavorings:** extra-virgin olive oil, raw apple cider vinegar, raw sesame oil, tamari

- **"Noodles":** kelp noodles, sweet potatoes, zucchini

- **Tea:** herbal infusions, hibiscus tea, white tea

- **Common veggies:** bell peppers, cabbage, carrots, cauliflower, kale

- **Common fruits:** avocados, berries, citrus fruits, tomatoes

More important than what's in your pantry, however, are the things you always have "going"—sprouting, fermenting, soaking, and so on. In raw cooking, it's essential to plan ahead, since many of the foods you eat need to be processed in some way to help your body get the nutrients it needs. For example, soaking raw nuts and seeds makes these vital protein sources more easily absorbed by the body, and fermented fruits and vegetables contain extra enzymes, B vitamins, omega-3 fatty acids, and probiotics that aid in digestive and overall health. On the same day I plan my menu for the week, I always take a few extra minutes to start a quick ferment and whip up a few essentials to save time later. For the easiest weekday meal plans, I recommend that you start the week as follows:

- Get at least one **lacto-ferment** in process. Sauerkraut (page 172) and Kimchi (page 175) are some of the most useful, but make whichever one you think you would use the most. See chapter 10 for more fermenting recipes.

- Make and refrigerate at least one **nut butter.** See pages 52, 163, and 165.

- Make at least one **nut milk.** See page 76.

- Peel, halve, and freeze **bananas** for use in smoothies.

- Start soaking at least one (and possibly several!) types of **nuts.** Soaking raw nuts and seeds removes anti-nutrients like phytates and tannins, neutralizes enzyme inhibitors, makes it easier for your body to absorb proteins, and gives these foods a texture that is easier to blend. Even if you have a high-speed blender—but especially if you don't—blending nuts can do a number on your blender blades. Soak the nuts for 8 to 10 hours before blending; you can soak buckwheat groats for less time, just 2 to 3 hours.

the raw deal on equipment

This is probably the part you were worried about. It's all well and good to promote the purchase of cheap fruits and vegetables, until you're also being told you need a $400 blender.

Well, that's not the case here. Pretty much everything you need is probably in your kitchen already. Sure, some plant-based and raw recipes do require specialty tools—for instance, you might decide to purchase a spiralizer if you find that you want to eat zoodles every day. But when you're just starting out, all you need are a few inexpensive tools:

- **BOX GRATER:** this everyday kitchen tool is all you need to make your own veggie noodles, cauliflower rice, and more.
- **VEGETABLE PEELER:** this is another indispensible tool for creating vegetable noodles, perfect for when you want a thicker noodle.
- **IMMERSION BLENDER:** starting at just $10, an immersion blender is an affordable alternative to a high-powered countertop blender that works great for smoothies and soups. Plus it will take up less space in your kitchen.
- **GOOD CHEF'S KNIFE:** this is the most important tool in your kitchen. Since you will be doing chopping of all kinds, it will be worthwhile to have a knife sharpener on hand as well.

And here are some tools and equipment you might need or want down the line, just to make things a bit simpler:

- **SPIRALIZER:** these handy tools help you make perfect vegetable noodles in a flash, and starting at just $10 for a simple hourglass model, they can be an inexpensive resource.
- **HIGH-POWERED BLENDER:** A Vitamix or Blendtec really is a game changer in the kitchen, but starting at more than $400, they aren't a practical purchase for most of us. Ninja, NutriBullet, and Oster offer more affordable high-speed blenders.
- **JUICER:** I love the juicer made by Jack LaLanne, and you can find great discounts for various models on Amazon.
- **MANDOLINE:** A mandolin will help you create perfectly

A SPOTLIGHT ON SPROUTING AND SOAKING

The two techniques that make raw nuts, seeds, beans, and legumes edible and digestible are soaking and sprouting. These related techniques accomplish two separate ends.

SOAKING is ideal for most nuts and seeds. If you soak nuts in fresh water for 24 hours ahead of using them, they will be softer and more malleable, ideal for transforming into nut milks and nut butters. Soaking is required in the case of certain seeds as well, such as chia seeds, whose gelling power is unleashed only after a soak in liquid.

SPROUTING is the raw foodie's trick to render grains, legumes, and certain seeds edible. You've likely already heard of mung bean sprouts, but you can also sprout spelt, lentils, peas, chickpeas, adzuki beans, and radish and broccoli seeds. You can even sprout nuts, if you're so inclined. Sprouting partially breaks down the food, making it easier for your digestive system to do the rest of the work—and helping your body absorb the nutrients sealed within.

Before sprouting, first thoroughly wash the containers you plan to use and rinse the seeds or beans under cool running water. Soak the seeds overnight in a bowl of

water at room temperature, rinse them well, and place the damp seeds in a sprouting bag or jar without any water. Place the bag or jar on your kitchen counter and rinse the seeds with fresh water every morning and night, keeping the sprouts wet but making sure no mold is growing on them. The seeds will begin to sprout anywhere from 1 to 5 days later, and then they're ready to eat. Rinse them well before using them in your desired dish. They should smell very clean or have no odor at all. If you ever notice an unpleasant odor coming from your sprouts, throw them out and start again.

sliced veggies in a flash, and can be purchased for under $20.

- NUT MILK BAGS: These reusable bags make it very simple to strain ground nuts when making nut milks. I recommend the Elaina Love nut bags.
- FOOD PROCESSOR: While a 4-cup food processor will get the job done for dips and sauces, you may want to invest in a 7- to 10-cup food processor, which will give you enough space to create great slaws, cauliflower rice, and more.
- DEHYDRATOR: Far from essential, dehydrators do yield the chewy texture of many comforting snacks and treats that you might crave on a raw food diet. None of the recipes in this book require a dehydrator and you can get away without one.

some tried-and-true formulas

This book is packed full of recipes for breakfasts, lunches, dinners, snacks, and even desserts. But these 100+ recipes are just the beginning. Ultimately, choosing a raw food diet means that you're going to have to start getting creative in the kitchen, and when you just can't be bothered to follow a recipe or you don't have time to head to the store, there are a few techniques you can use to whip up a quick meal with what you have on hand.

Think of the following ideas as guidelines that you can change up according to your tastes, your whims, or what you have in the pantry. Chapter 12 is a great resource for using dressings and sauces to add flavor to basic dishes like these, as well.

RAW PASTA

Soon, you're never going to be able to keep enough zucchini in the house. Why? Because zucchini can quickly and easily be transformed into pasta! Use the large holes on a box grater and grate the zucchini lengthwise to create spaghetti-like noodles, or use a vegetable peeler to create wider bands that resemble pappardelle. You may even want to invest in a spiralizer, which will give you more variety and make the process a little simpler.

Once you've got your zoodles, you can top them with all sorts of things, from diced tomatoes and basil for an Italian-inspired dish to chopped peppers and tamari for a more Asian flair. You can even just sprinkle them with nutritional yeast, black pepper, and a drizzle of olive oil for a raw take on *cacio e pepe*.

RAW BOWL

Buddha bowls have become common standbys for all kinds of dieters, but for raw foodies, they're essential. They're a great way to use up leftovers, as you can mix a variety of things in the same bowl. Just make sure that you're hitting all your bases: pick one protein-rich food like a leafy green or legume, one fattier food like nuts or avocado, and a bunch of different colored vegetables. Then whip up your favorite sauce from chapter 12, and dinner's ready!

RAW RICE

Use a box grater or food processor to turn cauliflower into a raw alternative to rice. Once you have this base, you can easily spice it up in many different ways. A "cheese" sauce (see page 126) can turn it into a risotto-like concoction, while an assortment of vegetables and a flavorful combo of lime juice, coconut sugar, tamari, and raw sesame oil can make it more like fried rice.

A RAW DAY IN THE REAL WORLD

When it comes to the day-to-day of your raw food diet, the most important thing is to listen to your body. Eat until you're full, and if you start to feel sluggish or tired, listen to those cues. Here is an idea of what a day in the real world of raw food might look like.

Morning
Start your day with a nutrient-packed, fresh green smoothie. Kale, broccoli, or spinach is the green portion, while any combo of fruits that strikes your fancy will add sweetness and even more vitamins. Drink your smoothie on an empty stomach, and be sure to "chew" so that the vitamins and minerals get absorbed as quickly as possible. Follow this up with a combination of

protein and carbohydrates. Chia pudding made with homemade almond milk takes care of the protein, while a topping of fresh fruit and a touch of raw honey add the carbs.

Afternoon

For lunch, you'll want something with fiber and protein to keep you satiated, as well as some carbs to get you through the rest of the day. And above all, you'll want to be sure that you keep your lunch as colorful as possible, to ensure that you're getting as many different vitamins and minerals as you can. Any one of the salads in chapter 6 is a good option; pick one that has a nut, a seed, or a dark leafy green to make sure that you hit the mark on protein.

Evening

After work, you might want a little snack. If you're really hungry, pick something protein-heavy, like Almond Butter–Stuffed Dates (page 165). If you just need an energy boost, opt for something a bit sweet, like a piece of fruit or a few On-the-Go Energy Bites (page 166).

For dinner, you can get a bit more creative. Choose something that's not only filling but also looks beautiful on the plate. Remember that we eat with our eyes first, so go for visual appeal with Raw Lasagna (page 136), Raw Pad Thai (page 124), or pretty Alfalfa Sprout Lettuce Wraps (page 128). Follow that up with a sweet dessert like Raw Chocolate-Avocado Pudding (page 183). When planning your dinnertime meals, always look out for dishes that are poorer in protein, and make up for them with nuttier desserts.

CHAPTER 3

THE RAW DEAL:
your 21-day meal plan

Let's face it: Meal plans are great in theory, but how often are they realistic? You might start the week with good intentions, only to find that you have to work late on Tuesday, or you didn't have time to get to the store on Thursday and all you can do is clean out the pantry.

The following framework is my response to every other raw food meal plan you'll find. It is designed to be simple and practical so that you can actually use it, and flexible to help make the transition to raw food easy. Follow these basic guidelines, and you'll slowly get used to "cooking" raw, with make-ahead breakfasts, lunches, and snacks, satisfying suggestions, and lots of wiggle room for leftovers, scheduling mishaps, and grocery store catastrophes. Always remember that no matter what happens, if you have a stocked pantry, you can always opt for zucchini noodles or cauliflower rice topped with whatever ferment or sprout you have going at the time and one of the sauces from chapter 12 to replace any of the meals on our suggested list.

raw breakfasts and lunches

For the first week of your new raw food regime, only breakfasts and lunches will be raw. For dinner, you should be eating steamed or poached lean proteins like fish or chicken, along with hearty helpings of vegetables and whole grains.

You've heard the old adage that breakfast is the most important meal of the day, and it's true for a number of reasons for the new "rawtarian." If you start things off with a raw breakfast, you'll be far more likely to commit to your raw lunch, whereas if you start things off on the wrong foot, it's tempting to feel that the day is "ruined" and that you should just start over tomorrow. So make it easy on yourself by being prepared: Write out your grocery list in advance, and be sure you have more than enough fruits, vegetables, and greens in your refrigerator for a raw smoothie in the morning. Yes, you'll be having a smoothie or a juice every morning alongside your breakfast; it's key to getting your digestion going and for making sure you get all your vitamins and minerals for the day.

Many of your breakfasts and lunches are easy to make in advance, so take the time to put those together the night before. You'll be far more inclined to grab a chia pudding or a salad jar if it's already in the refrigerator.

Sunday is going to be your big planning day. In addition to doing your grocery run, make a nice big batch of almond milk, which you'll be using in your almond milk chia puddings. You'll also need to start sprouting your chickpeas for the lunches near the end of the week and the raw falafel on Sunday. You can make your chia puddings and buckwheat breakfast cookies on Sunday, too, if you're worried you'll be strapped for time on weeknights.

The weekday lunches can all be prepared the night before and stored in mason jars for easy transportation to work. Just be sure to pour the dressing into the bottom of the jar, and pack lettuces and other tender ingredients at the top. When you're ready to eat, just shake the jar or dump it onto a plate.

Smoothies taste best straight from the blender, but if you know you'll be in a rush, you can make them the night before and store them in airtight containers in the refrigerator.

After a week's worth of easy recipes, you'll be trying some more technical recipes on the weekend. This will help you get prepared for next week, but don't worry—even the most complicated recipes in this book are easy to master.

	BREAKFAST	LUNCH
MONDAY	Green Monster Smoothie (PAGE 82) followed by Raw Almond Milk Chia Pudding with Blueberries and Pomegranate Seeds (PAGE 55)	Rainbow Salad (PAGE 92)
TUESDAY	Raw Kale and Carrot Juice (PAGE 71) followed by Buckwheat Breakfast Cookies (PAGE 63)	Kelp Noodle and Veggie "Stir-Fry" (PAGE 112)
WEDNESDAY	Mixed Berry Vita-Smoothie (PAGE 85) followed by Raw Almond Milk Chia Pudding with Blueberries and Pomegranate Seeds (PAGE 55)	Kale Summer Rolls with Satay Dipping Sauce (PAGE 151)
THURSDAY	Green Monster Smoothie (PAGE 82) followed by Buckwheat Breakfast Cookies (PAGE 63)	Mediterranean Salad (PAGE 98)
FRIDAY	Superfood Smoothie with Turmeric (PAGE 87) followed by Buckwheat Breakfast Cookies (PAGE 63)	Kale Superfood Salad with Sprouted Chickpeas (PAGE 90)
SATURDAY	Raw Virgin Mary (PAGE 74) followed by Raw Crêpes with Maple Syrup (PAGE 62)	Kelp Noodle Alfredo (PAGE 139)
SUNDAY	Pumpkin Spice Smoothie (PAGE 83) followed by Fake-Out Apricot "Fried Eggs" (PAGE 53)	Raw Falafel with Garlicky Dipping Sauce (PAGE 141)

Recommended Snacks

- Raw Broccoli Hummus (page 214) with carrot sticks
- 1 apple and a handful of soaked raw almonds
- 2 On-the-Go Energy Bites (page 166)
- Sweet Banana Ants-on-a-Log with Cinnamon Nut Butter and Cacao Nibs (page 163)
- Almond Butter–Stuffed Dates (page 165)

- Spicy Stuffed Avocado Halves (page 160)
- Perfect Guacamole (page 212) with zucchini slices
- Raw Almond Milk Chia Pudding with Blueberries and Pomegranate Seeds (page 55)
- Half an avocado with extra-virgin olive oil and Himalayan salt
- A small bowl of Sauerkraut (page 172)

raw breakfasts and lunches, and three raw dinners

By week two, you should be starting to identify the difference between real hunger and other feelings that you may have been mistaking for hunger before, like thirst or boredom. Over the course of a meal, try to pay attention to when you feel satiated, and seek to have that feeling, not a stuffed feeling, at the end of the meal. Depending on how raw you've gone this week, you might also be developing some flu-like symptoms or chills, which is completely normal. Try to boost your energy and your immune system with a smoothie or high-antioxidant snack.

This week, you'll eat many of the same breakfasts you enjoyed last week, freeing up time and mental energy to tackle the raw dinners you'll now be introducing to your routine. For the sprouted chickpeas, you can use some leftovers from last week or make some more. You'll want to get in the habit of always having some beans or pulses sprouting—this week, start a batch of lentils.

As with last week, you'll need to set aside an hour or two on Sunday to get some things out of the way. You can prepare your almond milk and your raw granola, and you can also make your chia parfait cream, sprouted seed flatbread, and cinnamon cashew butter in advance.

	BREAKFAST	LUNCH	DINNER
MONDAY	Green Monster Smoothie (PAGE 82) followed by Chia Parfait with Raw Granola (PAGE 58)	Rainbow Salad (PAGE 92)	Indian-Spiced Sprouted Chickpeas (PAGE 129)
TUESDAY	Raw Kale and Carrot Juice (PAGE 71) followed by Sprouted Flatbread with Fruit Purée (PAGE 60)	Kelp Noodle and Veggie "Stir-Fry" (PAGE 112)	
WEDNESDAY	Mixed Berry Vita-Smoothie (PAGE 85) followed by Chia Parfait with Raw Granola (PAGE 58)	Kale Summer Rolls with Satay Dipping Sauce (PAGE 151)	
THURSDAY	Green Monster Smoothie (PAGE 82) followed by Apples with Cinnamon–Cashew Butter Dip (PAGE 52)	Sweet and Savory Mexican Street Food Salad with Sprouted Green Lentils (PAGE 101)	
FRIDAY	Superfood Smoothie with Turmeric (PAGE 87) followed by Sprouted Flatbread with Fruit Purée (PAGE 60)	Sprouted Lentil Salad (PAGE 99)	Zoodles with Basil Pesto (PAGE 114)
SATURDAY	Hibiscus and Raw Raspberry Iced Tea (PAGE 67) followed by Mango-Coconut Breakfast Pudding (PAGE 54)	Fresh Pea Soup with Mint and Cashew Cream (PAGE 104)	Raw Lasagna (PAGE 136)
SUNDAY	Raw Chocolate Nut Milk (PAGE 78) followed by Rainbow Fruit Salad with Nuts (PAGE 50)	Cauliflower "Fried" Rice (PAGE 116)	

Recommended Snacks

- Savory Cucumber Ants-on-a-Log with Cashew "Cheese" and Goji Berries (page 156)
- Kale Chips (page 157)
- Mixed Berry Vita-Smoothie (page 85)
- 1 orange and a handful of soaked raw hazelnuts
- Raw Hummus with Za'atar and Pomegranate (page 213) with cauliflower florets

- Half an avocado with lime juice
- Half a cantaloupe
- Raw Kale and Carrot Juice (page 71)
- Buckwheat Breakfast Cookies (page 63)
- Half a banana with cinnamon almond butter

WEEK 3
7-day raw cleanse

By week three, you should be sleeping better and feeling more refreshed in the morning. You might also find that you're waking up before your alarm clock. It's possible that you'll be feeling some fairly intense cravings as well, so try to consider what it is you really want: If it's fried food, try eating something with healthy fat, like avocado. If it's chocolate, try out one of the desserts in chapter 11. And if it's something crisp and salty, kale chips should do the trick.

Now, the time has come for a whole week of raw food! A lot of this week's breakfasts and lunches will be things you've seen before, but there will be a few more things to prepare ahead. Keep those pulses sprouting—this week you'll need chickpeas and alfalfa sprouts. Also get some sauerkraut fermenting, as you'll be eating it as a side dish with several of the meals, and it's also nice to have on hand as a snack. You can make big batches of Pumpkin Spice Chia Pudding with Almonds (page 57) and Buckwheat Breakfast Cookies (page 63) on Sunday to enjoy throughout the week. And you can also make a bigger batch of Indian Spiced Sprouted Chickpeas (page 129) on Monday, as you'll be having them for dinner on Tuesday as well.

beyond the first 3 weeks

In the fourth week of your diet, you will set the framework for your new, balanced raw food lifestyle, based on how you feel and what works best for you. If you're really craving cooked food, try to resist eating heated foods for breakfast and lunch, and at dinnertime opt for gentle heating methods like steaming or poaching. It's important to take it slow if you want to reintroduce cooked foods—especially meat.

Most people who adhere to a raw food diet do not do so full time. If week 2 seemed doable for you, stick to that as a base plan, working with the idea of raw breakfasts and lunches all week long and just three raw dinners per week. If you'd rather scale it back even more, keep all of your breakfasts raw, eat raw lunches five times a week, and save raw dinners for the weekends only.

The most important thing to remember is to be prepared. If you keep your pantry stocked and continue to sprout beans and ferment different vegetables, you'll be able to eat as many raw recipes a week as you like.

	BREAKFAST	LUNCH	DINNER
MONDAY	Green Monster Smoothie (PAGE 82) followed by Pumpkin Spice Chia Pudding with Almonds (PAGE 57)	Cauliflower "Tabbouleh" Salad (PAGE 95)	Indian-Spiced Sprouted Chickpeas (PAGE 129)
TUESDAY	Superfood Smoothie with Turmeric (PAGE 87) followed by Buckwheat Breakfast Cookies (PAGE 63)	Kale and Mushroom Salad with Figs (PAGE 93)	Indian-Spiced Sprouted Chickpeas (PAGE 129)
WEDNESDAY	Green Monster Smoothie (PAGE 82) followed by Pumpkin Spice Chia Pudding with Almonds (PAGE 57)	Mediterranean Salad (PAGE 98)	Marinated Portobello Mushrooms with Fresh Tomato Stuffing (PAGE 121) and Sauerkraut (PAGE 172)
THURSDAY	Superfood Smoothie with Turmeric (PAGE 87) followed by Buckwheat Breakfast Cookies (PAGE 63)	Raw Pad Thai (PAGE 124)	Cauliflower Rice with "Cheese" Sauce (PAGE 126)
FRIDAY	Green Monster Smoothie (PAGE 82) followed by Pumpkin Spice Chia Pudding with Almonds (PAGE 57)	Mediterranean Salad (PAGE 98)	Raw Maque Choux (PAGE 130)
SATURDAY	Raw Virgin Piña Colada (PAGE 75) followed by Rainbow Fruit Salad with Nuts (PAGE 50)	Alfalfa Sprout Lettuce Wraps (PAGE 128) and Sauerkraut (PAGE 172)	Raw Lasagna (PAGE 136)
SUNDAY	PB&J Protein Smoothie (PAGE 86) followed by Fake-Out Apricot "Fried Eggs" (PAGE 53)	Avocado Taco Bowls (PAGE 122)	Raw Chili (PAGE 150) and Sauerkraut (PAGE 172)

Recommended snacks

- On-the-Go Energy Bites (page 166)
- Sauerkraut (page 172)
- Cacao Nib Truffles (page 192)
- Honey-Banana Ice Cream (page 185)
- Perfect Guacamole (page 212) with zucchini slices
- Superfood Smoothie with Turmeric (page 87)
- Raw Broccoli Hummus (page 214) with carrot sticks

the recipes

PART TWO

RAW ALMOND MILK
CHIA PUDDING WITH
BLUEBERRIES AND
POMEGRANATE SEEDS

CHAPTER 4

breakfast

rainbow fruit salad with nuts

SOY-FREE · UNDER 30 MINUTES

SERVES 2 · PREP: 15 MINUTES

1 orange, supremed (see Prep Tip), with juice

1 banana, peeled, halved lengthwise, and cut crosswise into half moons

1 peach, pitted and cut into wedges

1 kiwi, peeled, halved lengthwise, and cut crosswise into half moons

2 fresh figs, quartered

½ cup quartered fresh strawberries

½ cup fresh raspberries

½ cup fresh blueberries

½ cup fresh blackberries

¼ cup raw almonds, soaked for 8 hours, drained, and chopped

¼ cup raw hazelnuts, soaked for 8 hours, drained, and chopped

¼ cup hemp hearts, soaked for 8 hours and drained

What could be simpler than a beautiful fruit salad? This salad is loaded with vitamins and minerals, thanks to the multicolored ingredients, plus a bit of protein from the nuts. All in all, it's a super easy way to get a great jump start on your raw day. Hemp hearts, sometimes called shelled hemp seeds, can be found online or at specialty health food stores.

Toss all the ingredients together in a bowl; serve immediately.

PREP TIP: To supreme an orange or other citrus fruit, use a paring knife to remove all the skin and pith from the fruit. Next, carefully slice along the membrane on both sides of each segment; the segments should pop out with no membrane attached.

apples with cinnamon–cashew butter dip

SOY-FREE · UNDER $10 · UNDER 30 MINUTES

SERVES 2 · PREP: 15 MINUTES

2 cups raw cashews, soaked for 8 hours and drained

¼ cup unsweetened cashew milk, homemade (see page 79) or store-bought, plus more as needed

1 teaspoon ground cinnamon

½ teaspoon Himalayan salt

1 tablespoon raw honey

1 green apple, cored and sliced

1 red apple, cored and sliced

This quick and easy breakfast is even quicker and easier when you make the dip in advance. With this version, you'll end up with just under 2 cups of cashew butter, which you can keep in the refrigerator for up to a week and use on snacks and flatbreads.

1. Combine the cashews and cashew milk in a blender. Blend on high speed, scraping down the sides and adding more cashew milk as needed to achieve a smooth, thick consistency. The process may take as long as 10 minutes, and you will likely need to turn off the blender periodically to let it cool down.

2. When the cashew butter is relatively smooth, add the cinnamon and salt and continue to blend until you have a fairly smooth, dippable texture.

3. Scoop the cashew butter dip into a ramekin and drizzle the raw honey over the top. Serve the apples on a plate with the cashew butter dip.

PREP TIP: If you want to make a spreadable rather than dippable cashew butter, you'll need to use a food processor and omit the cashew milk completely.

fake-out apricot "fried eggs"

NUT-FREE · SOY-FREE · UNDER $10

SERVES 2 · PREP: 15 MINUTES · CHILLING: 30 MINUTES

Coconut oil, for greasing the ramekins

1 cup raw coconut milk, divided

1 teaspoon powdered agar-agar

3 tablespoons water

2 fresh apricots, halved and pitted

The "eggs" in this trompe-l'oeil dish are actually apricot halves placed on top of a thickened coconut gel made with agar-agar, a seaweed-based gelatin substitute.

1. Grease four small ramekins with coconut oil and set them aside. Pour ½ cup of the coconut milk into a medium bowl and set it aside.

2. Combine the agar-agar and water in a saucepan and bring to a boil. Boil for 3 minutes, whisking vigorously. Pour the remaining ½ cup coconut milk into the agar-agar and water mixture, continuing to whisk vigorously, then pour this combined mixture into the bowl with the reserved coconut milk. Immediately divide this mixture among the prepared ramekins. Set the ramekins in the refrigerator to chill until the agar-agar is set, about 30 minutes.

3. Remove the ramekins from the refrigerator and run a knife along the edges of the gelled coconut milk to remove it. Serve two coconut gel rounds on each plate; these will be the "egg whites." Place one apricot half on top of each coconut gel round, skin-side up. These are the "egg yolks." Serve the trompe l'oeil "fried eggs" immediately.

PREP TIP: For agar-agar to set, it must be brought to a boil, so it is technically not a raw food. However, many raw foodies include this gelatin substitute in their diets because it is a vegan food that offers the satisfaction of cooked desserts without the eggs and animal products.

mango-coconut breakfast pudding

NUT-FREE · SOY-FREE · UNDER 30 MINUTES

SERVES 2 · PREP: 15 MINUTES

1 cup chopped fresh
coconut meat, from
1 young Thai coconut

¼ cup fresh coconut water

1 tablespoon coconut sugar

1 banana, diced

1 mango, peeled, pitted,
and diced

2 tablespoons raw
unsweetened
coconut flakes

Most raw puddings use chia as a thickening agent, meaning that you have to wait a long time to reap the rewards. But this breakfast pudding is thickened with banana and coconut, giving it a slightly different texture but a much quicker result.

1. Combine the fresh coconut meat, coconut water, and coconut sugar in a blender and purée until smooth and creamy. Set aside.

2. Rinse out the blender and add the banana and mango. Blend until smooth and creamy.

3. In each serving bowl or glass, place a generous dollop of the coconut pudding, then a generous dollop of the banana-mango purée. Swirl the two together for a marbled effect. Top with a sprinkling of the raw coconut flakes and serve.

PLAN AHEAD: If you make the pudding a few hours in advance, you'll have time to chill it before serving, making it even thicker and creamier.

raw almond milk chia pudding with blueberries and pomegranate seeds

SOY-FREE

SERVES 2 · PREP: 15 MINUTES · CHILLING: OVERNIGHT

½ cup chia seeds

2 cups Raw Almond milk (see page 76) or store-bought, divided

3 tablespoons raw honey

½ teaspoon pure vanilla extract

¼ cup fresh blueberries

¼ cup pomegranate seeds

It's important to get both protein and carbs in your morning meal so you'll have enough energy to start the day and be able to stay full enough until lunchtime. But it can be tough to find something that fills those requirements and can also be prepared quickly when you're on the go. That's why these individual puddings are a great make-ahead breakfast. All you have to do in the morning is add the berries and eat!

1. The night before, combine the chia seeds and 1 cup of the almond milk in a bowl. Stir well and allow to sit for 10 minutes.

2. After 10 minutes, stir the mixture again, ensuring that the chia seeds are not sticking together. Add the remaining 1 cup almond milk, the raw honey, and the vanilla and stir well to make sure that everything is combined. Cover the bowl with plastic wrap and set in the refrigerator overnight.

3. In the morning, divide the chia pudding between two bowls. Divide the berries and pomegranate seeds evenly over the pudding and serve.

SUBSTITUTION: For a chocolaty breakfast treat, try using Raw Chocolate Nut Milk (page 78) instead of plain almond milk.

pumpkin spice chia pudding with almonds

SOY-FREE

SERVES 2 · PREP: 15 MINUTES · CHILLING: OVERNIGHT

½ cup chia seeds

2 cups Raw Almond Milk (see page 76) or store-bought, divided

2 tablespoons raw honey

1½ teaspoons ground cinnamon, divided

1 cup cubed pumpkin

1 tablespoon pure maple syrup

½ teaspoon ground ginger

½ teaspoon ground cloves

Freshly grated nutmeg

¼ cup raw almonds, chopped

¼ cup raw cacao nibs, chopped

Come fall, you'll be craving the warming spices of cinnamon, nutmeg, and cloves. This chia pudding is flavored with fall spices and pumpkin purée for a healthy, colorful treat packed full of beta carotene. Though maple syrup is not a raw product, I use it here to give the pudding some extra flavor. Feel free to substitute raw honey to keep this recipe 100 percent raw.

1. The night before, combine the chia seeds and 1 cup of the almond milk in a bowl. Stir well and allow to sit for 10 minutes.

2. After 10 minutes, stir the mixture again, ensuring that the chia seeds are not sticking together. Add the remaining 1 cup of almond milk, the raw honey, and ½ teaspoon of cinnamon and stir well to make sure that everything is combined. Cover the bowl with plastic wrap and set in the refrigerator overnight.

3. In the morning, combine the pumpkin, maple syrup, ginger, cloves, nutmeg, and remaining 1 teaspoon of cinnamon in a blender. Blend until smooth, drizzling in just enough water to achieve a purée.

4. Fold the pumpkin purée into the chia pudding. Divide the pudding into two glass jars or drinking glasses. Top with the chopped raw almonds and cacao nibs and serve.

SUBSTITUTION: This pudding is also delicious when made with hazelnut milk and hazelnuts.

chia parfait with raw granola

SOY-FREE

SERVES 2 · PREP: 15 MINUTES · DEHYDRATING: 4 HOURS · CHILLING: OVERNIGHT

FOR THE CHIA PUDDING

½ cup chia seeds

2 cups Raw Almond Milk
(page 76) or store-
bought, divided

2 tablespoons raw honey

FOR THE GRANOLA

1 cup raw buckwheat groats,
soaked for 2 hours
and drained

½ cup raw almonds, soaked
for 8 hours and drained

½ cup raw hazelnuts, soaked
for 8 hours and drained

½ cup raw unsweetened
coconut flakes

¼ cup raw cacao nibs

½ cup raw honey

2 tablespoons coconut oil

1 teaspoon ground
cinnamon

Raw granola is a classic beginner recipe for raw foodies because the raw version doesn't really taste all that different from the baked version. This parfait is a great make-ahead option, because both the chia pudding and the granola can be prepared in advance. Then, on a busy weekday morning, you can just grab it and go. Any leftover granola will keep in an airtight container at room temperature for up to 1 week.

TO MAKE THE CHIA PUDDING

1. The night before, combine the chia seeds and 1 cup of the almond milk in a bowl. Stir well and allow to sit for 10 minutes.

2. After 10 minutes, stir the mixture again, ensuring that the chia seeds are not sticking together. Add the raw honey and the remaining 1 cup almond milk and stir well to make sure everything is combined. Cover the bowl with plastic wrap and set in the refrigerator overnight.

TO MAKE THE GRANOLA

1. Also the night before, turn your oven to its lowest setting; if you have an oven thermometer, check to see that it doesn't go above 100°F. Line a baking sheet with parchment paper.

2. Stir together all the granola ingredients in a large bowl until well combined. Spread out the mixture on the lined baking sheet and place it in the oven. Prop open the oven door so that it does not overheat. Dehydrate until the granola sticks together in clumps, about 4 hours.

3. Transfer the granola to an airtight container lined with a paper towel or a kitchen towel to keep it from absorbing moisture in the air and losing its crunch.

4. The next morning, alternate layers of chia pudding with layers of granola in parfait glasses. You can also drizzle a bit more honey over the top before serving.

PREP TIP: If you live somewhere sunny, you can sun-dry your granola on a tray by the window. Just make sure to keep your granola in direct sunlight, and it will work just as well as a low-temperature oven.

sprouted flatbread with fruit purée

SOY-FREE

SERVES 2 · PREP: 20 MINUTES · DEHYDRATING: 5 HOURS

FOR THE FLATBREAD

½ cup flax seeds, soaked for
   10 minutes and drained

¾ cup sprouted buckwheat
   groats (see page 34)

½ cup raw almonds, soaked
   for 8 hours and drained

½ cup raw unsweetened
   coconut flakes

¼ cup sunflower seeds,
   soaked for 8 hours
   and drained

½ banana

Pinch Himalayan salt

FOR THE FRUIT PURÉE

10 fresh raspberries

10 fresh blueberries

5 fresh strawberries,
   quartered

5 fresh blackberries

Juice of ½ orange

Most raw "bread" recipes require the use of an expensive dehydrator, but with this one, you'll be using your oven. Don't worry—you won't be "cheating." If you set your oven to the very lowest setting and prop it open while this bread dries out, you won't do any damage to the food . . . and you won't have to buy a dehydrator either! The resulting flatbread has a great, nutty flavor and is perfect with a sweet fresh fruit purée.

TO MAKE THE FLATBREAD

1. Turn your oven to its lowest setting; if you have an oven thermometer, check to see that it doesn't go above 100°F. Line a baking sheet with parchment paper.

2. Put the flax seeds in a blender and blend until broken up and floury. Add the sprouted buckwheat, almonds, coconut, and sunflower seeds and run the blender until you have a sandy texture. Add the banana and salt and blend until combined.

3. Spread the dough evenly on the lined baking sheet. Place the bread in the oven and prop the door open so that it does not overheat. Dehydrate for 5 hours, then peel the bread from the baking sheet and set aside. If you are making the bread in advance, wrap it in a dishtowel and leave it on the countertop until ready to eat.

FOR THE FRUIT PURÉE

1. Combine all the fruit and the orange juice in a blender and blend until smooth.

2. Spread the purée over the flatbread and serve.

BLENDER BASICS

Using a blender for these sorts of mixtures can cause the motor to heat up and begin to cook the food. If you have a food processor, feel free to use it in any of the blender recipes in this book. If you don't have a food processor, be sure to stop the blender if it starts to heat up, and allow the motor to cool down before proceeding.

Once you find yourself making lots of raw recipes, keep track of whether you're using your blender more than five times a week. If you are, it might be worth investing in a high-powered blender, food processor, or perhaps both. Not only will you be able to mix doughs like these with ease, but you'll have an easier time getting your nut creams and nut milks to be smooth and creamy.

raw crêpes with maple syrup

NUT-FREE · SOY-FREE · UNDER $10

SERVES 4 · PREP: 15 MINUTES · DEHYDRATING: 3 HOURS

8 bananas

Juice of 1 lemon

Fresh sliced strawberries,
for serving

Pure maple syrup or raw
honey, for serving

When you started a raw diet, you probably thought that things like crêpes and pancakes were no more, but creatively minded rawtarians have discovered the ideal way to make crêpes—the secret is banana. These crêpes have a slightly denser texture when you take them out of the oven; I love them with maple syrup, which is not technically raw, but you can sub in nut butter instead if you're stricter than I am about your raw diet.

1. Turn your oven to its lowest setting; if you have an oven thermometer, check to see that it doesn't go above 100°F. Line a baking sheet with parchment paper.

2. Combine the bananas and lemon juice in a blender and blend until smooth. Add a little water as needed to help the mixture blend, but be aware that the more water you add, the longer you will need to dehydrate your crêpes.

3. Spread the batter evenly on the lined baking sheet. You should be able to make 8 crêpes. Place the crêpes in the oven and prop the door open so that it does not overheat. Dehydrate until the crêpes no longer stick to your fingers when you touch them, about 3 hours. Do not overdo it! They will have a texture close to fruit leather when done.

4. Peel the crêpes from the parchment paper and place on plates. Fold in half and serve with the strawberries and a drizzle of maple syrup.

buckwheat breakfast cookies

SOY-FREE

MAKES 50 · PREP: 20 MINUTES · CHILLING: 1 HOUR

1 cup raw buckwheat groats, soaked for 2 hours and drained

1 cup sunflower seeds, soaked for 3 hours and drained

1 cup raw almonds, soaked for 8 hours and drained

1 cup raw unsweetened shredded coconut

½ cup agave nectar

½ cup raw honey

½ cup coconut oil

Himalayan salt

It's always a good idea to have a few to-go breakfasts in your raw food arsenal. Throw together these buckwheat breakfast cookies on a weekend morning and you'll have them on hand all week long. Filled with healthy fats, fiber, and protein, they're a great way to get a jump on your day.

1. Put the buckwheat groats in a blender and blend until they are reduced to a floury texture. Transfer to a mixing bowl. Repeat with the sunflower seeds, almonds, and coconut. Stir together all four flours in the bowl.

2. Drizzle in the agave, honey, and coconut oil. Knead the dough with your hands until it comes together. You may have to add more agave or coconut oil if the dough is too sandy. Season the dough with salt.

3. Line a baking sheet with parchment paper. Make small balls of dough and flatten them out on the lined baking sheet. Chill for 1 hour before serving, and store any leftovers in the refrigerator.

CHAPTER 5

beverages

basil lemonade with blueberries

NUT-FREE · SOY-FREE · UNDER $10 · UNDER 30 MINUTES

SERVES 2 · PREP: 15 MINUTES

2 cups cold water

1 cup freshly squeezed
    lemon juice

½ cup raw honey

8 basil leaves, divided

24 fresh blueberries, divided

What's more refreshing than a cool glass of lemonade? This raw version also boasts the antioxidants of blueberries and the summery flavor of basil. Muddling the blueberries gives the lemonade a beautiful purple color that makes this drink even more pleasing to sip.

In a pitcher, stir together the water, lemon juice, and honey. Place 3 basil leaves and 7 blueberries in each glass and muddle with a wooden spoon. Add ice and pour the lemonade over the top. Garnish each glass with 1 basil leaf and 5 blueberries and serve.

hibiscus and raw raspberry iced tea

NUT-FREE · SOY-FREE · UNDER $10

SERVES 4 · PREP: 5 MINUTES · CHILLING: OVERNIGHT

½ cup dried hibiscus flowers

4 cups cold water

1 cup fresh raspberries

4 lime wedges, for garnish

Hibiscus tea has a beautiful red color and a slightly pungent, floral flavor. It is used around the world for its health benefits, including easing digestion, maintaining blood pressure, and supporting lung and skin health. This cold-brewed tea with raspberries will also help keep sugar cravings at bay.

In a pitcher, combine the hibiscus flowers and the cold water. Cover and refrigerate overnight. When ready to serve, muddle ¼ cup of raspberries in each glass and pour the tea over the top. Serve garnished with the lime wedges.

raw white tea with peaches and rosemary

NUT-FREE · SOY-FREE · UNDER $10

SERVES 4 · PREP: 5 MINUTES · CHILLING: OVERNIGHT

½ cup raw white tea

2 sprigs fresh rosemary, divided

4 cups cold water

2 peaches, sliced in eighths

Most teas are dried and processed in ways that make them incongruous with a fully raw diet, but not so with some white teas. White tea is basically raw green tea, and it contains many of the same catechins and other benefits that are touted by green tea. When combined with fresh peaches and rosemary, it makes a refreshing drink for summertime.

1. In a pitcher, add the white tea and the cold water. Stir to combine. Add 1 sprig of rosemary and cover. Refrigerate overnight.

2. In the morning, strain out the tea leaves and rosemary and discard. Add the peaches and a few small bunches of rosemary needles, and return the container to the refrigerator until ready to serve. The longer you allow the peaches to infuse, the more color and flavor they will lend to the tea. But do not surpass 24 hours or they may become waterlogged.

iced chai

SOY-FREE · UNDER $10

SERVES 2 · PREP: 15 MINUTES · CHILLING: OVERNIGHT

1 (2-inch-long) piece fresh ginger, peeled and chopped

10 whole cloves

6 cardamom pods, crushed

2 cinnamon sticks, bruised

2 teaspoons whole black peppercorns

½ cup coconut sugar

6 white tea teabags

6 cups cold water

2 cups Raw Almond Milk (page 76) or store-bought

Chai is a traditional Indian drink made of warm spices, tea, and milk. This version uses raw white tea, though you could also forgo the tea entirely and just make it a slightly sweet spice infusion instead. This sweet treat is a healthy addition to your raw food lifestyle: Cinnamon is high in antioxidants and polyphenols and has been proven to reduce blood sugar and have anti-inflammatory, antiviral, antifungal, and antibacterial properties. Ginger has anti-inflammatory and digestive benefits, and white tea contains metabolism-boosting catechins and antioxidants.

Combine all the ingredients in a large pitcher and stir. Cover and place in the refrigerator overnight. Stir once more before straining. Serve over ice.

raw kale and carrot juice

NUT-FREE · SOY-FREE · UNDER $10 · UNDER 30 MINUTES

SERVES 2 · PREP: 15 MINUTES

4 carrots, peeled and grated

10 kale leaves,
    finely chopped

¼ cup water

If you don't have a juicer, you might think it's impossible to make raw juices at home, but you'd be wrong! You can make your own raw juices with a bit of help from your blender and some cheesecloth.

1. Combine the carrots, kale, and water in a blender. Blend, stopping as needed to allow the blender motor to cool down, until you have a fairly even purée.

2. Place two layers of cheesecloth over a bowl or pitcher and pour the veggie purée through the cheesecloth. Wring the cheesecloth over the container until you have removed all the juice from the pulp. Pour into glasses and serve immediately.

PLAN AHEAD: Be sure to save the wrung-out veggie scraps from the cheesecloth; the scraps can be added to your next Buddha bowl for extra fiber.

raw spinach, avocado, and kiwi smoothie

NUT-FREE · SOY-FREE · UNDER $10 · UNDER 30 MINUTES

SERVES 2 · PREP: 15 MINUTES

2 cups spinach leaves, finely chopped

1 avocado

2 kiwis, peeled and chopped

1 lime, divided

This smoothie gets its great texture from avocado and a touch of sweetness from kiwi. The more green smoothies you drink, the less you will have a need for the added sugar of fruit, so feel free to reduce the amount of kiwi you add as you make this smoothie over and over again.

1. Combine the spinach, avocado, and kiwi in the blender. Add the juice of half of the lime and blend, stopping as needed to scrape down the sides, until everything is smoothly combined.

2. Slice rounds of lime from the second half of the fruit and place them on the edges of the glasses as a garnish. Pour in the smoothie and serve.

virgin sunrise cocktail

NUT-FREE · SOY-FREE · UNDER $10

SERVES 2 · PREP: 15 MINUTES · CHILLING: OVERNIGHT

½ cup fresh strawberries

½ cup water

3 tablespoons chia seeds

Juice of 1 orange

1 mango, peeled, pitted, and cubed

This beautiful beverage is perfect for serving in the evening when you get home from work as a pick-me-up, or even first thing in the morning with breakfast. To keep the two liquids relatively separate, you'll need to make sure that they're of different densities, thus the use of the chia seeds to thicken the strawberry mixture.

1. Combine the strawberries and water in a blender and blend until completely smooth. Transfer the strawberry purée to a bowl and add the chia seeds. Cover and refrigerate overnight.

2. When ready to prepare your cocktails, put a spoonful of the strawberry chia gel in the bottom of each glass. Combine the orange juice and mango in a blender and blend until smooth. Add water as needed to thin out the liquid slightly so that it is easily pourable. Pour the mango juice over the chia gel and watch as the colors combine for a sunrise in each glass.

raw virgin mary

NUT-FREE · UNDER $10 · UNDER 30 MINUTES

SERVES 2 · PREP: 15 MINUTES

4 tomatoes, chopped

3 celery stalks, 1 chopped
and 2 left whole
for garnish

1 lemon, ½ juiced and ½ cut
into wedges for garnish

1 teaspoon tamari

1 teaspoon raw apple
cider vinegar

Pinch cayenne pepper

When you think about it, this perennial brunch favorite is actually good for you—as long as you exclude the alcohol. This raw cocktail is chock-full of vitamins, nutrients, and flavor.

Combine the tomatoes, chopped celery, lemon juice, tamari, cider vinegar, and cayenne in a blender and blend until smooth. Fill the glasses with ice cubes and pour the mixture over the ice. Serve garnished with celery stalks and lemon wedges.

DIY HACK: Spice up your Raw Virgin Mary with home-made Habanero Hot Sauce—see page 203 for the recipe.

raw virgin piña colada

NUT-FREE · SOY-FREE · UNDER $10 · UNDER 30 MINUTES

SERVES 2 · PREP: 5 MINUTES

1 cup diced frozen
    pineapple

1 cup chopped fresh
    coconut meat, from 1
    young Thai coconut

¼ cup fresh coconut water

1 tablespoon coconut sugar

Alcohol is definitely a no-no on raw, but that doesn't mean you can't have a virgin cocktail. This raw version of a piña colada uses coconut and pineapple for a thick, icy treat you can enjoy any time of day. The only thing you'll have to remember to do in advance is freeze the pineapple chunks.

Combine the frozen pineapple, coconut meat, coconut water, and coconut sugar in a blender and blend until smooth. Serve immediately.

PREP TIP: If you've forgotten to freeze the pineapple chunks, simply make it a piña colada smoothie.

raw almond milk

SOY-FREE

MAKES 4 CUPS · PREP: 15 MINUTES · SOAKING: 2 DAYS

2 cups raw almonds

4 cups water, plus more
for soaking

Once you go raw, you'll notice yourself enjoying a variety of nut milks—both on their own and in all sorts of dishes—so it's nice to have a fresh batch in the refrigerator when you need it. I try to whip up a recipe of almond milk at least once or twice a week. Not only is it cheaper than the store-bought stuff, but it's a lot tastier and healthier, too. Once you get the hang of it, I recommend treating yourself to a nut milk bag, a large, reusable fabric pouch that makes straining a breeze.

1. Put the almonds in a large glass bowl and cover them with water by about 2 inches. Cover the bowl with plastic wrap and soak in the refrigerator for 2 days, topping off the water as needed.

2. When the soaking is done, drain the almonds and rinse them well. The almonds should feel a bit spongy and springy in texture. Combine the almonds and 4 cups of fresh water in a blender and blend, pulsing first and then blending for a full 3 minutes on the blender's highest speed, until the almonds are completely broken down.

3. If you have a nut milk bag, slowly pour the liquid through the bag into a large bowl or basin. If you haven't yet invested in a nut milk bag, you can use cheesecloth. To do this, place two layers of cheesecloth loosely over a jar so that some of the cheesecloth is hanging down into the jar. Secure the cheesecloth to the rim of the jar with a rubber band. You will end up with a pocket of cheesecloth hanging into the jar. Slowly pour the liquid through the cheesecloth pocket into the jar.

4. When you have poured all the liquid through the bag or cheesecloth, squeeze and press the bag or cheese-cloth until all the liquid is extracted. Store the almond milk in a covered container in the refrigerator for up to 2 days.

PLAN AHEAD: Once your almond milk is strained, save the leftover almond meal for use in any recipe that calls for almond meal or almond flour. Just be sure that it's completely dry before you store it: Spread it out on a baking sheet and allow it to dry at room temperature. Then place it in a sealed container and store it in the refrigerator for up to a week.

raw chocolate nut milk

SOY-FREE

MAKES 4 CUPS · PREP: 15 MINUTES · SOAKING: 2 DAYS

2 cups raw cashews

¼ cup raw cacao nibs

4 cups water, plus more
for soaking

2 tablespoons raw
cocoa powder

2 tablespoons raw honey

Missing this childhood favorite on the raw diet? You're in luck—there's no need to miss out on chocolate milk. This recipe is delicious just for sipping, but you may also want to keep some chocolate nut milk around to add to your chia puddings for even more chocolate flavor.

1. Put the cashews and cacao nibs in a large glass bowl and cover them with water by about 2 inches. Cover the bowl with plastic wrap and soak in the refrigerator for 2 days, topping off the water as needed.

2. When the soaking is done, drain the cashews and cacao nibs and rinse well. The cashews should feel a bit spongy and springy in texture. Combine the cashews, cacao nibs, and 4 cups of fresh water in a blender and blend, pulsing first and then blending for a full 3 minutes on the blender's highest speed, until the cashews and cacao nibs are completely broken down.

3. If you have a nut milk bag, slowly pour the liquid through the bag into a large bowl or basin. If you haven't yet invested in a nut milk bag, you can use cheesecloth. To do this, place two layers of cheesecloth loosely over a jar so that some of the cheesecloth is hanging down into the jar. Secure the cheesecloth to the rim of the jar with a rubber band. You will end up with a pocket of cheesecloth hanging into the jar. Slowly pour the liquid through the cheesecloth pocket into the jar.

4. When you have poured all the liquid through the bag or cheesecloth, squeeze and press the bag or cheese-cloth until all the liquid is extracted.

5. Put the cocoa powder in a pitcher and whisk in the cashew milk, tablespoon by tablespoon, until you have a thin paste with no lumps. Add the rest of the cashew milk slowly, whisking all the while. Sweeten with honey and serve.

OTHER VARIETIES OF NUT MILK

Almond milk is a favorite among raw foodies, thanks to its relatively mild flavor. But there are plenty of other nuts that you can use to make milk, including raw cashews, raw hazelnuts, raw macadamia nuts, and raw pistachios. Coconuts make great milk as well, although technically not a nut, and are a wonderful option if you're nut-free. The ratio of 2 cups raw nuts to 4 cups water can be used for most nuts, though when using a fattier nut like cashews or macadamia nuts, you may need to add a bit more water to the blender to achieve the right consistency. Follow the directions given for Raw Almond Milk (page 76) to make any other nut milk.

berry-mint smoothie

NUT-FREE · SOY-FREE · UNDER $10 · UNDER 30 MINUTES

SERVES 2 · PREP: 15 MINUTES

2 cups fresh raspberries

1 cup fresh blackberries

½ frozen banana, chopped

5 mint leaves

½ cup freshly squeezed
    orange juice

1 teaspoon flax seeds

This summery smoothie is super easy to drink and digest. While it doesn't offer a lot of variety in terms of vitamins and minerals, it is a delicious treat and rich in antioxidants. It's particularly good as a snack or dessert; if you drink it first thing in the morning, you'll need to be sure to get some protein into your breakfast for a good balance.

Combine all the ingredients in a blender and blend until smooth. Serve immediately.

green monster smoothie

NUT-FREE · SOY-FREE · UNDER $10 · UNDER 30 MINUTES

SERVES 2 · PREP: 5 MINUTES

10 kale leaves, torn

1 mango, peeled, pitted, and cubed

1 (1-inch) piece fresh ginger, peeled

1 avocado, peeled, pitted, and cubed

1 frozen banana, chopped

Smoothies are essential to a raw food diet. You can consume the quantity of vitamins and minerals that you need much more easily in smoothie form than by just eating fruit or salad, and starting your day with fresh fruit and vegetables really jump-starts your metabolism. To get the most out of your smoothie, be sure to "chew" it as you drink it. Digestion starts in the mouth, so while it might seem strange at first, you'll soon find that it's much easier to digest your smoothie if you chew before swallowing.

Place all the ingredients in a blender and blend until smooth. If needed, you can add some water or freshly squeezed orange juice to help the blender turn more easily.

SUBSTITUTION: A green smoothie allows you to get lots of vegetables in along with your fruits. You can change up the ingredients, subbing spinach or broccoli for the kale and any fruit you like for the mango. Pick a fruit with a strong aroma like pineapple or berries to help balance out the flavors of the vegetables.

pumpkin spice smoothie

SOY-FREE · UNDER 30 MINUTES

SERVES 2 · PREP: 15 MINUTES

3 cups unsweetened
   hazelnut milk,
   homemade (see page 79)
   or store-bought

2 cups cubed fresh pumpkin

1 tablespoon raw honey

1 (½-inch) piece fresh
   ginger, peeled

1 teaspoon ground
   cinnamon

½ teaspoon ground cloves

Freshly grated nutmeg

This delicious fall smoothie is a great breakfast booster, as it is chock-full of beta carotene. The ginger and cinnamon are great for your immune system and help give you energy first thing in the morning.

Combine all the ingredients in a blender and blend until smooth. Serve immediately.

DIY HACK: There's no need to use a peeler or knife to remove the skin from a piece of fresh ginger. Use a spoon instead to scrape it away, leaving the flesh intact.

mixed berry vita-smoothie

NUT-FREE · SOY-FREE · UNDER 30 MINUTES

SERVES 2 · PREP: 15 MINUTES

1 cup quartered fresh
strawberries

1 cup fresh raspberries

1 cup fresh blueberries

1 cup fresh blackberries

1 cup fresh red currants

½ frozen banana

Juice of 1 orange

When you're feeling a bit under the weather, nothing can boost you more than fresh berries and citrus. This vita-smoothie is perfect for mornings when you're feeling a bit sluggish or feel you might be coming down with a cold.

Combine all the ingredients in a blender and blend until smooth. Serve immediately.

SUBSTITUTION: Red currants offer a refreshingly sweet acidity to this smoothie, but if you can't find them, you can substitute fresh pitted cherries for a richer, deeper flavor.

pb&j protein smoothie

SOY-FREE · UNDER $10 · UNDER 30 MINUTES

SERVES 2 · PREP: 15 MINUTES

½ cup hemp hearts, soaked for 8 hours and drained

½ cup almonds, soaked for 8 hours and drained

½ frozen banana, chopped

1 tablespoon coconut sugar

Pinch Himalayan salt

½ cup fresh strawberries

This smoothie is a great boost right after a workout to help your muscles repair themselves. While reminiscent of the childhood favorite sandwich, this smoothie actually contains no peanuts; unlike almonds and other nuts, peanuts are very difficult to digest when raw, as they're not actually a nut at all but a legume. Hemp hearts and almonds form the nutty portion of this smoothie, which is swirled with a strawberry "jam" purée.

1. Combine the hemp hearts, almonds, banana, coconut sugar, and salt in a blender. Blend, drizzling in water as needed, until smooth. Pour the smoothie into a pitcher and rinse out the blender.

2. Put the strawberries in the blender and blend until smooth.

3. Pour about one-fourth of the smoothie into each glass and top with about one-fourth of the strawberry purée. Use a spoon to swirl the purée into the smoothie for a marbled effect. Top with the rest of the smoothie, and finish with the rest of the strawberry purée. Swirl once more and serve with a straw.

superfood smoothie with turmeric

SERVES 2 · PREP: 15 MINUTES

1 mango, peeled, pitted, and diced

½ frozen banana, chopped

1 cup chopped fresh coconut meat, from 1 young Thai coconut

Juice of 1 orange

¼ cup coconut water

1 tablespoon chia seeds

1 tablespoon ground turmeric

Before you started raw, you likely had turmeric only in curry, but this superfood has been proven to be one of the most beneficial medicinal plants in the world, according to Chris Kilham, the "Medicine Hunter." Its bright yellow color makes it the perfect addition to this orange smoothie.

Combine all the ingredients in a blender and blend until smooth. Allow to sit for at least 10 minutes before drinking to allow the chia to work its magic.

KALE AND MUSHROOM SALAD WITH FIGS

CHAPTER 6

salads & soups

kale superfood salad
with sprouted chickpeas

SOY-FREE · UNDER 30 MINUTES

SERVES 2 · PREP: 10 MINUTES

2 tablespoons extra-virgin
    olive oil

1 tablespoon freshly
    squeezed lemon juice

1 teaspoon agave nectar

Himalayan salt

Freshly ground
    black pepper

1 bunch kale, large stems
    removed, leaves
    roughly chopped

1 cup sprouted chickpeas
    (see page 34)

2 teaspoons flax seeds

½ cup raw
    almonds, chopped

½ cup dried cranberries

Salads can be iffy to prepare in advance and bring to work, but kale salads are different. Whereas other lettuces tend to wilt when they spend too much time in the refrigerator, kale salads can actually benefit from a bit of marinating time, which breaks down the fibrous crucifer and makes it easier and more pleasant to eat and digest.

1. In a large bowl, whisk together the olive oil, lemon juice, and agave. Season with salt and pepper. Add the kale and massage the vinaigrette into the kale with your fingers for 30 to 45 seconds. This will tenderize and collapse the kale a bit.

2. Top the kale with the sprouted chickpeas, flax seeds, raw almonds, and dried cranberries. Serve.

PLAN AHEAD: If you're making this salad to be transported, massage the kale with the dressing, then place it in the bottom of a mason jar or other container and top with the remaining ingredients. This will prevent the more tender items from getting too soggy.

marinated mushroom salad

NUT-FREE · SOY-FREE

SERVES 2 · PREP: 10 MINUTES · MARINATING: 30 MINUTES

2 tablespoons extra-virgin
olive oil, divided

1½ tablespoons freshly
squeezed lemon
juice, divided

1 garlic clove, minced

Himalayan salt

Freshly ground
black pepper

1 pound cremini
mushrooms, cut into ¼-
to ½-inch-thick slices

8 ounces baby spinach

½ bunch parsley,
finely chopped

1 red onion, thinly sliced

Mushrooms are one of the ingredients that you need to be a bit wary about when eating raw. Some health professionals claim that they can be dangerous, which is why I prefer to marinate them first, as a kind of ceviche.

1. In a large bowl, whisk together 1 tablespoon of olive oil, 1 tablespoon of lemon juice, the garlic, salt, and pepper. Add the mushroom slices and toss well to coat them all. Set aside to marinate for 30 minutes, tossing occasionally.

2. When the mushrooms are marinated, whisk together the remaining 1 tablespoon of olive oil and ½ table-spoon of lemon juice in another large bowl. Add the mushrooms and any remaining marinade and toss. Add the spinach, parsley, and red onion and toss until well combined. Serve immediately.

rainbow salad

NUT-FREE · SOY-FREE · UNDER 30 MINUTES

SERVES 2 · PREP: 20 MINUTES

8 ounces baby spinach

½ red cabbage, thinly sliced

1 red bell pepper, seeded and thinly sliced

1 yellow bell pepper, seeded and thinly sliced

2 carrots, peeled and cut into ribbons with a vegetable peeler

3 scallions, dark green parts thinly sliced crosswise, white and light green parts thinly sliced lengthwise

½ cup fresh blueberries

2 tablespoons grapeseed oil

1 tablespoon raw apple cider vinegar

1 teaspoon raw honey

1 teaspoon Dijon mustard

Himalayan salt

Freshly ground black pepper

1 avocado, peeled, pitted, and quartered

2 fresh figs, quartered

You eat with your eyes first, but that's not the only reason you should include lots of different colors on your plate. A variety of colors in your fruits and vegetables translates to a variety of nutrients; this salad will hit loads of vitamin and mineral bases in just one meal.

1. In a large bowl, combine the spinach, cabbage, bell peppers, carrots, scallions, and blueberries.

2. In a small bowl, whisk together the grapeseed oil, cider vinegar, raw honey, and Dijon mustard. Season with salt and pepper. Add the vinaigrette to the bowl of vegetables and toss well to combine. Top with the avocado and figs. Serve immediately.

PREP TIP: Making ribbons of harder vegetables such as carrots and sweet potatoes can be a great way to integrate them into raw food dishes. Just remove the outer skin with a vegetable peeler, then keep "peeling" thick ribbons until you get to the center. This also works for zucchini if you don't have a spiralizer.

kale and mushroom salad with figs

SOY-FREE

SERVES 2 · PREP: 40 MINUTES

3 tablespoons extra-virgin olive oil, divided

2 tablespoons freshly squeezed lemon juice, divided

1 garlic clove, minced

Leaves stripped from 1 thyme sprig

1 pound white button mushrooms, cut into ¼- to ½-inch-thick slices

1 teaspoon Dijon mustard

Himalayan salt

Freshly ground black pepper

1 bunch kale, large stems removed, leaves roughly chopped

4 fresh figs, quartered

½ cup raw hazelnuts, chopped

This is one of my favorite fall salads, especially when I am thinking of the dishes I used to make on the Standard American Diet. This salad, with the rich flavors of the mushrooms, the sweetness of the figs, and the alkalinity of the kale, is a fantastic, filling salad for fall that really delivers.

1. In a large bowl, whisk together 1 tablespoon of olive oil, 1 tablespoon of lemon juice, garlic, and thyme. Add the mushroom slices and toss well to coat them all. Set aside to marinate for 30 minutes, tossing occasionally.

2. When the mushrooms are marinated, whisk together the remaining 2 tablespoons of olive oil, 1 tablespoon of lemon juice, and mustard in another large bowl and season with salt and pepper. Add the kale and massage the vinaigrette into the kale with your fingers for 30 to 45 seconds. This will tenderize and collapse the kale a bit.

3. Top the kale with the marinated mushrooms and any remaining marinade, the figs, and the hazelnuts. Serve immediately.

cauliflower "tabbouleh" salad

NUT-FREE · SOY-FREE · UNDER $10 · UNDER 30 MINUTES

SERVES 2 · PREP: 20 MINUTES

1 cauliflower head, cut
   into florets

Juice of 1 lemon, plus ½
   lemon for garnish

Himalayan salt

1 medium tomato,
   finely diced

¼ cucumber, finely diced

1 bunch parsley, cut into
   chiffonade (see Prep Tip)

10 mint leaves, cut into
   chiffonade (see Prep Tip)

1 tablespoon extra-virgin
   olive oil

Freshly ground
   black pepper

In this recipe, grated cauliflower stands in for the bulgur wheat used in traditional tabbouleh. Marinating the cauliflower in acid is a trick that breaks down some of the harder-to-digest elements of the vegetable, making it much more pleasant to eat—in terms of both flavor and digestion. If you don't have a food processor, you can easily prepare the cauliflower with a box grater. In that case, don't cut the cauliflower into florets; just quarter the head so you'll have larger pieces to hold on to as you grate.

1. Work in batches to make the cauliflower "bulgur." Put the cauliflower florets in the food processor, but fill the bowl only about two-thirds of the way. Pulse the cauliflower to the size of rice grains. As you pulse, some pieces may remain whole while others have already become rice. It's important to remove any big chunks and set aside the remaining rice as you go so that you don't end up with a paste. Continue with the rest of the florets. Then, at the end, return all the big chunks to the food processor and pulse so that you have processed the whole head of cauliflower. (If the core of the cauliflower is tender, you can use it as well.) ››

cauliflower "tabbouleh" salad

CONTINUED

2. Transfer the cauliflower rice to a bowl, add the lemon juice, and season with salt. Fluff with a fork. Add the tomatoes; the acid in the tomatoes will help break down the cauliflower even further. Set aside to marinate for 5 to 10 minutes.

3. Add the cucumber, parsley, mint, and olive oil and season with pepper. Gently toss the tabbouleh with a fork to combine, making sure not to crush the cauliflower. Garnish with lemon wedges. Serve immediately.

PREP TIP: Cutting herbs into a chiffonade keeps them from oxidizing and darkening. To do this, use a very sharp knife. Lay fresh herb leaves one on top of the other and roll them into a tube. Slice the tube crosswise as thinly as possible so that you end up with ribbons of herb.

tomato and raw corn summer salad

NUT-FREE · SOY-FREE · UNDER $10 · UNDER 30 MINUTES

SERVES 2 · PREP: 10 MINUTES

4 ears corn, kernels cut from the cobs, corn milk reserved

4 medium heirloom tomatoes, chopped, juices reserved

½ bunch basil, cut into chiffonade (see Prep Tip, page 96)

2 tablespoons extra-virgin olive oil

Pinch Himalayan salt

Sweet corn and vine-ripened tomatoes are the stars of summer, and here they shine together in all their glory. Choose a variety of different heirloom tomatoes and multicolored corn to make this salad even more colorful. And no matter what you do, never keep fresh, whole tomatoes in the refrigerator; the cold temperature will weaken their flavor.

In a large bowl, combine the corn kernels and the milk scraped from the cobs with the tomatoes and all their juices. Add the basil and olive oil, season with salt, and toss together until just combined. Serve.

PREP TIP: This salad improves in flavor as it rests, so it's a great choice for make-ahead lunches. Just leave out the basil and add it to the salad right before you eat.

mediterranean salad

NUT-FREE · SOY-FREE · UNDER 30 MINUTES

SERVES 2 · PREP: 10 MINUTES

2 tablespoons extra-virgin olive oil

1 tablespoon freshly squeezed lemon juice

1 garlic clove, minced

1 cup sprouted chickpeas (see page 34)

1 heirloom tomato, chopped

½ English cucumber, chopped

1 red onion, thinly sliced

10 pitted olives

15 basil leaves, cut into chiffonade (see Prep Tip, page 96)

Himalayan salt

Freshly ground black pepper

Leaves stripped from 1 thyme sprig

1 teaspoon dried oregano

1 teaspoon nutritional yeast

Here is my raw food answer to Greek salad. The combination of textures and flavors is so satisfying, I promise you won't miss the feta and anchovies. For best results, chop the tomato and cucumber so they are the same size as the chickpeas. Not only will this make for a prettier salad, but it will also ensure that all the ingredients are equally incorporated.

1. In a large bowl, whisk together the olive oil, lemon juice, and garlic. Add the chickpeas, tomato, cucumber, red onion, olives, basil, and season with salt and pepper. Toss together until well combined.

2. Sprinkle the thyme, oregano, and nutritional yeast over the top of the salad. Serve immediately.

sprouted lentil salad

NUT-FREE · SOY-FREE · UNDER $10 · UNDER 30 MINUTES

SERVES 2 · PREP: 10 MINUTES

2 cups sprouted lentils (see page 34)

1 cup arugula

2 carrots, peeled and diced

1 tablespoon raw tahini

Juice of 1 lime

1 teaspoon ras el hanout

1 garlic clove, minced

1 avocado, peeled, pitted, and quartered

Arils from 1 pomegranate

Himalayan salt

Freshly ground black pepper

I love the earthy flavor of sprouted lentils. In this dish, their flavor is highlighted with a Middle Eastern–flavored dressing and a good amount of healthy fat. This is a great dish to plan on a day when you know you'll be extra hungry, as both the lentils and avocado have staying power, making you feel fuller longer.

1. In a large bowl, toss together the lentils, arugula, and carrots.

2. In a small bowl, whisk together the tahini, lime juice, ras el hanout, and garlic. Drizzle the dressing over the top of the salad, then toss to combine.

3. Top the salad with the avocado quarters and pomegranate arils, and season with salt and pepper. Serve immediately.

DIY HACK: You can easily make your own ras el hanout spice blend by mixing equal parts ground cardamom, ground mace, ground ginger, ground nutmeg, ground allspice, ground cinnamon, ground cloves, ground black pepper, and ground nigella seed.

sweet-and-sour red cabbage salad

NUT-FREE · SOY-FREE · UNDER $10

SERVES 2 · PREP: 10 MINUTES · DRAINING AND RESTING: 1 HOUR

1 red cabbage, thinly sliced

Himalayan salt

2 tablespoons grapeseed oil

2 tablespoons raw apple
cider vinegar

1 tablespoon agave nectar

2 tablespoons
coconut sugar

1 teaspoon caraway seeds

Freshly ground
black pepper

1 red onion, thinly sliced

2 tablespoons chopped
fresh parsley

Cabbage can be a little tough to eat raw, but when it's marinated in a sweet vinegar solution, German-style, it develops a deliciously delicate texture. Enjoy this salad as an entrée, or toss it into your next Buddha bowl. And always feel free to double the recipe, since it only gets better with age.

1. Put the red cabbage in a colander and season it with a hefty pinch of salt. Allow it to drain for 40 minutes.

2. After 40 minutes, press the cabbage to release as much water as possible.

3. In a large bowl, whisk together the grapeseed oil, cider vinegar, agave, coconut sugar, caraway seeds, and season with salt and pepper. Add the red onion and the drained cabbage and toss well to combine. Set aside for 20 minutes.

4. Toss the salad once again, then top with the chopped parsley and serve.

sweet and savory mexican street food salad with sprouted green lentils

NUT-FREE · SOY-FREE · UNDER $10 · UNDER 30 MINUTES

SERVES 2 · PREP: 10 MINUTES

12 romaine leaves, chopped

1 cup sprouted green lentils (see page 34)

1 orange, supremed (see Prep Tip, page 50)

1 jicama, julienned (see Prep Tip, page 153)

1 green apple, cored and julienned (see Prep Tip, page 153)

1 mango, peeled, pitted, and diced

1 tablespoon extra-virgin olive oil

1 bunch cilantro, chopped

Juice of 1 lime

Chili powder

Himalayan salt

Inspired by a Mexican street food treat, this salad entices the taste buds with a mixture of sweet and spicy flavors. Serve it with lime wedges and extra chili powder for those who like it hot.

In a large bowl, toss together the romaine, lentils, orange, jicama, apple, mango, and olive oil. Top with the cilantro and lime juice and season with chili powder and salt. Serve.

SUBSTITUTION: While this salad makes for a delicious meal on its own, I also love to serve it as little romaine "boat" hors d'oeuvres. In that case, buy baby romaine leaves instead of regular romaine, and stuff them with the rest of the salad ingredients.

raw pumpkin soup

SOY-FREE · UNDER $10 · UNDER 30 MINUTES

SERVES 2 · PREP: 20 MINUTES

1 small pumpkin, peeled
  and cubed

3 cups unsweetened
  hazelnut milk,
  homemade (see page 79)
  or store-bought, divided,
  plus more for garnish

Freshly ground nutmeg

1 teaspoon ground
  cinnamon

½ teaspoon ground cloves

½ teaspoon ground ginger

Himalayan salt

Freshly ground
  black pepper

This soup is evocative of all the flavors, aromas, and colors of fall. While pumpkin is the standby, other winter squashes can be substituted in this soup as well. Red kuri squash is a great choice thanks to its light chestnut aroma, which pairs particularly well with the hazelnut milk.

1. Combine the pumpkin and half of the hazelnut milk in a blender. Blend on low speed until the pumpkin is relatively broken down, then add the rest of the hazelnut milk, nutmeg, cinnamon, cloves, ginger, and season with salt and pepper. Blend until completely smooth.

2. Serve in bowls topped with a dollop of hazelnut milk and freshly ground black pepper.

PLAN AHEAD: Be sure to rinse and reserve the pumpkin seeds, which can be used in other recipes. To make them crispy, let them dehydrate slightly in a low oven or on a sunny windowsill.

fresh pea soup with mint and cashew cream

SOY-FREE · UNDER $10 · UNDER 30 MINUTES

SERVES 2 · PREP: 20 MINUTES

½ cup raw cashews, soaked for 8 hours and drained

2 to 3 tablespoons water

2 tablespoons extra-virgin olive oil, divided

1 tablespoon freshly squeezed lemon juice

Himalayan salt

Freshly ground black pepper

4 cups fresh peas

2 cups unsweetened cashew milk, homemade (see page 79) or store-bought, divided

8 fresh mint leaves, 6 whole and 2 cut into chiffonade (see Prep Tip, page 96)

In the spirit of a gazpacho, this cold, raw soup is perfect for spring. Use the freshest peas you can find, and feel free to dress it up with other toppings, like sprouted chickpeas, chopped cashews, or a bit of spice.

1. Put the cashews in a blender and add 2 tablespoons of water, 1 tablespoon of olive oil, and the lemon juice. Blend until a smooth cream forms, adding another 1 tablespoon of water if needed. Transfer to a bowl and season with salt and pepper. Rinse out the blender.

2. In the blender, combine the peas, 1 cup of cashew milk, the remaining 1 tablespoon of olive oil, and the whole mint leaves. Blend until relatively smooth. Continue drizzling in the remaining 1 cup of cashew milk until you reach the consistency you'd like for your soup.

3. Serve the soup in bowls topped with a dollop of cashew cream and the mint chiffonade, as well as a touch more black pepper.

raw gazpacho

SOY-FREE · UNDER $10 · UNDER 30 MINUTES

SERVES 2 · PREP: 10 MINUTES

½ cup raw almonds, soaked
    for 8 hours and drained

1 shallot, chopped

1 garlic clove, chopped

6 tomatoes, peeled, seeded
    and chopped

3 tablespoons extra-virgin
    olive oil, plus more
    for garnish

1 red bell pepper, seeded
    and chopped

½ cucumber, seeded
    and chopped

1 tablespoon raw apple
    cider vinegar

Himalayan salt

Freshly ground
    black pepper

Chopped fresh parsley,
    for garnish

Gazpacho is already nearly raw—the only thing you're missing in a raw version is the thickening factor of the bread. For that, we borrow from an authentic but lesser-known version of this cold soup, white gazpacho, which gets its body from almonds.

1. Put the almonds, shallot, garlic, and tomatoes in a blender. Blend until relatively smooth, adding a little of the olive oil as needed to help the blender turn.

2. Add the bell pepper and cucumber to the blender. Run it on low speed, drizzling in the rest of the olive oil and the cider vinegar. Season with salt and pepper.

3. When the soup is smooth, serve in bowls topped with the chopped parsley and an extra drizzle of extra-virgin olive oil.

green gazpacho

SOY-FREE · UNDER $10 · UNDER 30 MINUTES

SERVES 2 · PREP: 20 MINUTES

¼ cup raw almonds, soaked for 8 hours and drained

½ cup Raw Almond Milk (page 76)

2 tablespoons extra-virgin olive oil

1 tablespoon raw apple cider vinegar

1 avocado, peeled, pitted, and quartered

½ English cucumber, chopped

½ green bell pepper, chopped

1 large tomatillo, husked and chopped

1 scallion, sliced

1 jalapeño, seeded and chopped

1 garlic clove, chopped

Himalayan salt

Chopped fresh chives and/or parsley, for garnish

While not as famous as its red counterpart, green gazpacho is a classic in its own right. It's got a bit of a sharper flavor due to the jalapeño and green bell pepper, but the avocado adds a smooth creaminess that gives this soup texture and staying power.

1. Combine all the ingredients (except the herb garnish) in a blender and blend until smooth. Add more almond milk or olive oil as needed if the blender does not blend easily.

2. Serve in bowls garnished with chopped fresh chives and/or parsley.

creamy raw corn bisque

SOY-FREE · UNDER $10 · UNDER 30 MINUTES

SERVES 2 · PREP: 20 MINUTES

4 ears corn, kernels cut from
 the cobs, corn milk
 reserved

1 shallot, chopped

2 cups Raw Almond Milk
 (page 76)

½ red bell pepper,
 finely diced

1 tomato, peeled and
 seeded, finely diced

Himalayan salt

Freshly ground
 black pepper

Fresh thyme

While bisques are typically on the heavy side, this creamy raw version has all the sumptuous texture without the overly rich heft. Be sure to use only the freshest seasonal corn for this dish—it's the star, after all.

1. In a blender, combine the corn kernels and the milk scraped from the cobs. Add the shallot. Begin to blend and slowly drizzle in the almond milk. Blend until you have a creamy consistency; depending on your corn, you may not need all the almond milk.

2. Pour the soup into bowls and add the bell pepper and tomato. Stir to combine. Season with salt, pepper, and fresh thyme and serve.

spinach soup with garlic and coconut

NUT-FREE · SOY-FREE · UNDER 30 MINUTES

SERVES 2 · PREP: 20 MINUTES

1 clove garlic

4 cups baby spinach, plus some leaves reserved for garnish

1 can coconut milk

Himalayan salt

Freshly ground black pepper

¼ cup fresh coconut shavings

1 pinch turmeric

This soup is rich and creamy, but it's also absolutely full of nutrients. Spinach is one of the best vegetarian sources of iron out there, and when it's combined with the antibacterial and antifungal properties of garlic and the healthy fats of coconut, it comes together in a marriage of flavors and nutrients. It doesn't hurt that it's super simple to make, too.

1. Peel the garlic clove, halve it, and remove the sprout. Soak the garlic clove in cold water for 10 minutes.

2. Remove the garlic clove from the water and add it to a blender bowl along with most of the spinach and the coconut milk. Blend, adding water as needed, until the soup is very smooth and slightly frothy. Season with salt and pepper.

3. Pour the soup into bowls and top with the reserved spinach leaves, the coconut shavings, and the pinch of turmeric. Serve.

RAW BEET CARPACCIO WITH
SALSA VERDE

weeknight entrées

kelp noodle and veggie "stir-fry"

NUT-FREE · UNDER 30 MINUTES

SERVES 2 · PREP: 20 MINUTES

2 cups kelp noodles, rinsed very well in warm water and drained

1 red bell pepper, seeded and julienned (see Prep Tip, page 153)

1 carrot, peeled and cut into long strips with a peeler

10 sugar snap peas, very thinly sliced lengthwise

½ cup bean sprouts

½ red chile pepper, seeded and very thinly sliced

1 tablespoon tamari

1 tablespoon raw sesame oil

1 tablespoon grapeseed oil

1 tablespoon raw honey

1 tablespoon raw apple cider vinegar

1 garlic clove, minced

1 (¼-inch) piece fresh ginger, peeled and grated

There are certain things you start to miss on a raw food diet, and complex carbs are one of them. Thankfully, there are some great pasta substitutes out there that are suitable for a raw food diet. Kelp noodles look a lot like spaghetti but have a very different texture. In this Asian-influenced noodle dish, they add a fun chewiness that contrasts with the crunchy texture of raw veggies. Just don't get too addicted—kelp noodles are made with iodine-rich seaweed, so you shouldn't eat them more than three times a week.

1. In a large bowl, combine the kelp noodles, bell pepper, carrot, snap peas, bean sprouts, and chile.

2. In a small bowl, whisk together the tamari, sesame oil, grapeseed oil, honey, and vinegar. Taste the dressing for balance and correct as needed. Whisk in the garlic and ginger.

3. Add the dressing to the bowl of noodles and vegetables and toss to coat. Allow to marinate for 5 minutes before serving.

PREP TIP: Chiles are a popular ingredient in raw food because they can add heat to a dish without any cooking. That being said, however, they can easily overpower a recipe if you add too much. If you want a little less heat, remove the seeds, ribs, and membranes of a chile before adding it to a recipe. Also, be sure to taste the pepper before adding it to the dish, as heat can vary even within the same variety of pepper. Wash your hands very well after cutting chiles, as the oils can continue to burn your skin long after the prep work is over.

zoodles with basil pesto

SOY-FREE · UNDER $10 · UNDER 30 MINUTES

SERVES 2 · PREP: 20 MINUTES

FOR THE PASTA

2 large zucchini, cut
     into noodles

Himalayan salt

FOR THE PESTO

4 tablespoons raw pine nuts

1 garlic clove, halved

2 tablespoons
     nutritional yeast

2 cups fresh basil leaves

½ cup extra-virgin olive oil

Himalayan salt

Freshly ground
     black pepper

This raw play on an Italian classic is super simple to make. It uses zucchini noodles as the pasta base and a raw pesto sauce as a topping. You can feel free to add a bit of spinach to the basil to get some iron into this dish, or just enjoy it as is. Be sure to eat it soon after preparing, or the zoodles will begin to give off water and may make the pasta sauce too loose.

TO MAKE THE PASTA

Put the zoodles in a strainer and sprinkle with a little bit of salt. Allow to sit for 10 minutes, then pat dry with a paper towel.

TO MAKE THE PESTO

1. Combine the pine nuts, garlic, and nutritional yeast in a blender and pulse a few times to break up the garlic clove and pine nuts. Add the basil leaves and a drizzle of olive oil. Blend on low speed, slowly drizzling in the remaining olive oil, until the pesto is smooth. Do not overblend, or you risk oxidizing the basil. Season the pesto with salt and pepper.

2. Spread some pesto on each plate, and add the rest to the zoodles. Toss gently to combine, then place the pasta on top of the layer of pesto. Serve immediately.

DIY HACK: You don't need to buy a spiralizer to make vegetable noodles; they can be made with either a box grater or a peeler. A box grater will make noodles more like spaghetti, while a peeler will yield results more like pappardelle. To make noodles with a box grater, grate the zucchini lengthwise, so you end up with noodles that are as long as possible.

cauliflower "fried" rice

UNDER 30 MINUTES

SERVES 2 · PREP: 25 MINUTES

1 cauliflower head, cut
    into florets

Juice of 1 lime

3 tablespoons tamari

2 tablespoons grapeseed oil

1 tablespoon coconut sugar

1 garlic clove, minced

1 cup fresh green peas

1 zucchini, finely diced

½ pineapple, finely diced

2 hot red chile peppers,
    seeded and minced

½ bunch cilantro, chopped

3 scallions, thinly sliced

½ cup macadamia
    nuts, chopped

This "fried" rice dish combines a few different influences. The flavors are evocative of a Thai noodle dish, with lime and crushed nuts, but the texture is definitely closer to a Chinese fried rice dish. Together, it's satiating and flavorful . . . and it's also just a starting point. Once you have this base recipe, it's easy to change it up depending on the veggies you have on hand. Feel free to make it your own.

1. Work in batches to make the cauliflower rice. Put the cauliflower florets in the food processor, but fill the bowl only about two-thirds of the way. Pulse the cauliflower to the size of rice grains. As you pulse, some pieces may remain whole while others have already become rice. It's important to remove any big chunks and set aside the remaining rice as you go so that you don't end up with a paste. Continue with the rest of the florets. Then, at the end, return all the big chunks to the food processor and pulse so that you have processed the whole head of cauliflower. (If the core of the cauliflower is tender, you can use it as well.)

2. In a large bowl, whisk together the lime juice, tamari, grapeseed oil, coconut sugar, and garlic. Taste the dressing for balance and correct as needed. Add the rice to the bowl with the dressing and fluff with a fork. Set aside to marinate for 5 to 10 minutes.

3. Add the peas, zucchini, pineapple, and chiles to the rice. Toss to combine.

4. Plate the cauliflower "fried" rice and top with the cilantro, scallions, and macadamia nuts. Serve immediately.

DIY HACK: If you don't have a food processor, you can use a box grater to make your cauliflower rice. Quarter the cauliflower and, holding it by the stem end, grate on the large grating holes. The cauliflower may begin to crumble as you get down to the base of the florets; only grate for as long as you can keep your fingers safe. Reserve any remaining pieces and toss them onto your next Buddha bowl.

butternut tagliatelle
with raw spinach-basil pesto

SERVES 2 · PREP: 20 MINUTES

1 butternut squash,
    quartered lengthwise
    and seeded

Himalayan salt

4 tablespoons raw pine nuts

1 garlic clove, halved

1 tablespoon
    nutritional yeast

1 cup basil leaves

1 cup baby spinach

½ cup extra-virgin olive oil

Freshly ground
    black pepper

Sweet winter squash stands in for tagliatelle in this faux pasta dish, and a quick blender pesto makes a simple topping. The spinach in this pesto adds iron to the dish, which is a mineral you need to be aware of on raw. Just 1 cup of spinach has 0.8 milligram iron, which contributes to your recommended dietary allowance.

1. To make the butternut squash tagliatelle, use a vegetable peeler to peel long ribbons of the flesh. Play with the pressure you use to find a thickness that you like. Stop when you get to the outer peel.

2. Put the butternut tagliatelle in a colander and season with a hefty pinch of salt. Set aside to drain slightly while you make the pesto.

3. Combine the pine nuts, garlic, and nutritional yeast in a blender and pulse a few times to break up the garlic clove and pine nuts. Add the basil leaves and spinach and a drizzle of olive oil. Blend on low speed, slowly drizzling in the remaining olive oil, until the pesto is smooth. Do not overblend, or you risk oxidizing the basil. Season the pesto with salt and pepper.

4. Transfer the butternut tagliatelle to a bowl and add a few tablespoons of pesto. Toss to coat. Plate the butternut tagliatelle and top with a few more spoonfuls of pesto. Serve immediately.

SUBSTITUTION: You can also make this pesto with arugula, for a bit of a spicier flavor, or with baby kale for something earthier. If you have any leftover cashew béchamel or savory cashew "cheese" lying around, it makes a great topping for this dish.

mango, cucumber, and wasabi nut summer roll

SERVES 2 · PREP: 40 MINUTES

4 rice paper wrappers

1 mango, julienned (see Prep Tip, page 153)

1 cucumber, julienned (see Prep Tip, page 153)

Juice of 1 lime

1 teaspoon grapeseed oil

½ cup baby arugula

6 mint leaves, cut into chiffonade (see Prep Tip, page 96)

¼ cup raw green tea wasabi nuts, crushed

This dish technically isn't 100 percent raw, as rice paper wrappers are made from cooked rice. That said, they are a healthy food that can be easily used with a mostly raw diet. If you're trying to stick to only raw foods with this recipe, try making these into lettuce wraps instead.

1. Prepare the rice paper wrappers for use according to package instructions.

2. Toss the mango, cucumber, lime juice, and grapeseed oil together in a bowl.

3. Assemble the spring rolls: start with a thin layer of arugula, and top with a stack of julienned cucumber and mango, all of the pieces facing the same way. Top with a bit of mint and a sprinkling of wasabi nuts, and fold the summer rolls so that the julienne is parallel to the seam of the roll. Serve alone or with one of our sauces. The Spicy Tahini Sauce (page 210) would be a great pairing.

marinated portobello mushrooms with fresh tomato stuffing

SERVES 2 · PREP: 15 MINUTES · MARINATING: 1 HOUR

1 tablespoon extra-virgin olive oil

1 tablespoon raw apple cider vinegar

1 garlic clove, minced

4 portobello mushroom caps

4 fresh tomatoes, chopped

2 sun-dried tomatoes, minced

1 kale leaf, minced

½ cup almond meal, left over from making Raw Almond Milk (page 76)

1 teaspoon tamari

While you can easily just add almond meal (or any other nut meal left from making nut milk) to your breakfast pudding or lunchtime Buddha bowl, this recipe gives you a slightly more creative way to use it up. Here, it helps bind together a delicious, Mediterranean-inspired stuffing for portobello mushrooms, adding rich, bready flavor and extra protein, too.

1. In a large bowl, whisk together the olive oil, cider vinegar, and garlic. Add the mushroom caps and toss to coat well. Marinate for 1 hour, turning occasionally.

2. Meanwhile, put the tomatoes in a strainer over a bowl and allow their excess liquid to drain off for about 20 minutes. (Reserve the tomato juice for another recipe.) In a bowl, combine the drained tomatoes, sun-dried tomatoes, kale, almond meal, and tamari. Toss to mix well.

3. When the portobello mushroom caps have finished marinating, pat them dry and fill them with the tomato stuffing. Serve 2 caps per person.

avocado taco bowls

SOY-FREE · UNDER 30 MINUTES

SERVES 4 · PREP: 20 MINUTES

FOR THE "REFRIED" BEANS

¼ cup cashews, soaked for 8 hours and drained

1 tomato, chopped

1 garlic clove, halved

1 teaspoon ground cumin

1 teaspoon ground coriander

1 cup sprouted adzuki beans (see page 34)

Himalayan salt

Freshly ground black pepper

FOR THE TOMATO PICO DE GALLO

2 tomatoes, diced

1 white onion, minced

1 jalapeño, seeded and minced

Himalayan salt

To me, the best thing about taco night was always assembling my own personalized plate, with lots of toppings to choose from. That's the idea behind these raw taco bowls. Just serve everyone a plate with two lime-scented avocado halves, and let them pile on their own beans and salsas.

TO MAKE THE "REFRIED" BEANS

Combine the cashews, tomato, garlic, cumin, and coriander in a blender and blend until creamy. Transfer the mixture to a bowl, add the sprouted adzuki beans, and season with salt and pepper.

TO MAKE THE TOMATO PICO DE GALLO

Combine the tomatoes, onion, and jalapeño. Season with salt.

FOR THE MANGO SALSA

1 mango, peeled, pitted, and diced

1 red onion, minced

1 red banana chile pepper, seeded and minced

½ bunch cilantro, finely chopped

Juice of 1 lime

Himalayan salt

FOR THE TACO BOWLS

4 avocados

Juice of 1 lime

TO MAKE THE MANGO SALSA

In a small bowl, combine the mango, red onion, banana chile, cilantro, and lime juice. Season with salt.

TO MAKE THE TACO BOWLS

Halve the avocados and remove the pits. Squeeze the lime juice over the cut sides of the avocados. Serve 2 avocado halves per person, along with the bowls of "refried" beans, pico de gallo, and mango salsa and let each person make their own taco bowls.

SUBSTITUTION: You can substitute pineapple for mango in the salsa, depending on your preference and what's available.

raw pad thai

UNDER 30 MINUTES

SERVES 2 · PREP: 15 MINUTES

¼ cup tamari

2 tablespoons grapeseed oil

2 tablespoons raw
sesame oil

1 tablespoon water

1 garlic clove, minced

1 tablespoon tamarind
paste or chopped fresh
tamarind

2 tablespoons
coconut sugar

1 zucchini, cut into ribbons
with a vegetable peeler

1 carrot, peeled and cut into
ribbons with a
vegetable peeler

5 scallions, thinly sliced

2 cups mung bean sprouts

½ bunch cilantro, chopped

½ cup raw macadamia nuts,
chopped, for garnish

1 Thai chile, seeded and
thinly sliced, for garnish

Lime wedges, for garnish

Pad thai offers a fantastic combination of flavors, and it's fairly easy to replicate raw. In this version, the quantities of mung beans are increased as compared to a more traditional pad thai, as they add crunch and texture to the dish.

1. In a small bowl, whisk together the tamari, grapeseed oil, sesame oil, water, garlic, tamarind, and coconut sugar. Set aside the mixture for 10 minutes.

2. Combine the zucchini, carrot, scallions, mung bean sprouts, and cilantro in a large bowl.

3. When the dressing has sat for 10 minutes, taste it and adjust the seasoning as needed. Strain it to remove the pieces of tamarind. Pour the dressing over the vegetables and toss to combine.

4. Serve the pad thai garnished with the macadamia nuts, chile slices, and lime wedges.

PREP TIP: Raw macadamia nuts do not have the same enzyme inhibitors as other nuts and therefore are perfectly healthy to eat unsoaked.

cauliflower rice with "cheese" sauce

SOY-FREE · UNDER $10 · UNDER 30 MINUTES

SERVES 2 · PREP: 15 MINUTES

1 cauliflower head, cut
    into florets

Himalayan salt

2 cups raw cashews, soaked
    for 8 hours and drained

1 red bell pepper, seeded
    and chopped

½ to 1 cup water

¾ cup nutritional yeast

2 tablespoons raw apple
    cider vinegar

1 garlic clove, chopped

2 teaspoons ground
    turmeric

Freshly ground
    black pepper

This dish is my version of raw risotto, with creamy cashew "cheese" sauce enrobing little grains of cauliflower "rice." And though it may look pale in color—a rarity among raw food meals—it's bursting with bright and earthy flavors.

1. Work in batches to make the cauliflower rice. Put the cauliflower florets in the food processor, but fill the bowl only about two-thirds of the way. Pulse the cauliflower to the size of rice grains. As you pulse, some pieces may remain whole while others have already become rice. It's important to remove any big chunks and set aside the remaining rice as you go so that you don't end up with a paste. Continue with the rest of the florets. Then, at the end, return all the big chunks to the food processor and pulse so that you have processed the whole head of cauliflower. (If the core of the cauliflower is tender, you can use it as well.)

2. Transfer the cauliflower rice to a strainer, add a hefty pinch of salt, and set aside while you make the sauce.

3. Put the cashews and bell pepper in a blender and add a bit of water to help them blend. Purée until a paste forms. Add the nutritional yeast, cider vinegar, garlic, and turmeric and continue to blend until smooth, adding more water as needed until you get a creamy consistency. Season with salt and pepper.

4. Transfer the cauliflower rice to a bowl, toss with the "cheese" sauce, and serve immediately.

cajun-spiced sprouted adzuki beans and cauliflower rice

NUT-FREE · SOY-FREE · UNDER $10 · UNDER 30 MINUTES

SERVES 2 · PREP: 25 MINUTES

1 head cauliflower, cut into florets

1 tablespoon raw apple cider vinegar

3 meaty heirloom tomatoes, roughly chopped

1 shallot, chopped

1 garlic clove, chopped

Leaves stripped from 1 marjoram sprig

Leaves stripped from 1 thyme sprig

1 teaspoon paprika

1 teaspoon cayenne pepper

1 cup sprouted adzuki beans (see page 34)

1 green bell pepper, seeded and finely chopped

Himalayan salt

Freshly ground black pepper

1 scallion, thinly sliced

This recipe is inspired by traditional Louisiana red beans and rice. The raw tomato sauce is flavored with Cajun spices and then tossed with sprouted adzuki beans, which stand in for kidney beans. For an extra kick, serve it with Habanero Hot Sauce (page 203).

1. Work in batches to make the cauliflower rice. Put the cauliflower florets in the food processor, but fill the bowl only about two-thirds of the way. Pulse the cauliflower to the size of rice grains. As you pulse, some pieces may remain whole while others have already become rice. It's important to remove any big chunks and set aside the remaining rice as you go so that you don't end up with a paste. Continue with the rest of the florets. Then, at the end, return all the big chunks to the food processor and pulse so that you have processed the whole head of cauliflower. (If the core of the cauliflower is tender, you can use it as well.)

2. Transfer the cauliflower rice to a bowl, add the cider vinegar, and set aside to marinate while you prepare the beans.

3. Combine the tomatoes, shallot, garlic, marjoram, thyme, paprika, and cayenne in a blender and blend until smooth. In a large bowl, combine the fresh tomato sauce, the sprouted adzuki beans and the green bell pepper. Season with salt and pepper.

4. Serve the adzuki beans over the rice, garnished with the sliced scallion.

alfalfa sprout lettuce wraps

NUT-FREE · SOY-FREE · UNDER $10 · UNDER 30 MINUTES

SERVES 2 · PREP: 5 MINUTES

1 avocado, peeled, pitted, and sliced

1 orange, supremed (see Prep Tip, page 54)

Juice of 1 lime

10 butter lettuce leaves

2 cups alfalfa sprouts

When you need something super quick, super tasty, and super filling, this is the recipe to come to. There's barely any work involved, and you end up with a delicious and fun-to-eat lunch or dinner.

In a bowl, toss the avocado slices and orange supremes with the lime juice. Pile a bit of filling into each lettuce leaf and top with alfalfa sprouts. Roll up and eat.

SUBSTITUTION: While alfalfa sprouts are easy to find and use, any kind of sprout will work in this recipe. Use whatever you have on hand, and take note of the ones you like the best.

indian-spiced sprouted chickpeas

SOY-FREE · UNDER 30 MINUTES

SERVES 2 · PREP: 10 MINUTES

3 cups sprouted chickpeas
(see page 34)

1 red bell pepper, seeded
and finely diced

1 tomato, finely diced

½ cup cashews, soaked for 8
hours and drained

1 garlic clove, halved

1 tablespoon grapeseed oil

1 teaspoon ground turmeric

1 teaspoon ground cumin

1 teaspoon ground
coriander

½ teaspoon cayenne pepper

¼ teaspoon ground ginger

¼ teaspoon ground
cinnamon

1 to 3 tablespoons water

Himalayan salt

Freshly ground
black pepper

Chopped fresh cilantro,
for garnish

Sprouted chickpeas are the base for this dal-inspired dish. Change up the spices to suit your own preferences, if you like, and pair it with cauliflower rice for an extra-filling meal.

1. In a bowl, combine the sprouted chickpeas, red bell pepper, and tomato.

2. Combine the cashews, garlic, grapeseed oil, turmeric, cumin, coriander, cayenne, ginger, and cinnamon in a blender. Add 1 tablespoon of water and blend, adding more water as necessary, until you have a creamy sauce.

3. Pour the sauce over the vegetables and toss to combine. Season with salt and pepper, sprinkle with cilantro, and serve.

PLAN AHEAD: Make a double batch and enjoy it throughout the week. These spiced chickpeas will keep for up to 5 days in an airtight container in the refrigerator.

raw maque choux

NUT-FREE · SOY-FREE · UNDER $10 · UNDER 30 MINUTES

SERVES 2 · PREP: 10 MINUTES

4 ears corn, kernels cut from the cob and divided, corn milk reserved

1 green bell pepper, seeded and finely diced

1 tomato, finely diced

1 scallion, finely diced

Himalayan salt

Freshly ground black pepper

Cayenne pepper

1 garlic clove, minced

Maque choux is a traditional dish from Louisiana made of braised corn and other vegetables. In this version, the ingredients are kept raw, of course, and sweet corn milk stands in for the broth.

1. In a bowl, combine the corn kernels from 3 of the 4 ears, the bell pepper, the tomato, and the scallion. Season with salt, pepper, and cayenne.

2. Combine the reserved corn milk and the remaining corn kernels in a blender. Add the garlic and blend until smooth.

3. Toss the corn sauce with the maque choux. Serve immediately.

PREP TIP: The corn milk is essential to this dish; you can get it easily by running the edge of your knife along the cobs after the kernels are removed.

raw beet carpaccio with salsa verde

NUT-FREE · SOY-FREE · UNDER 30 MINUTES

SERVES 2 · PREP: 10 MINUTES

FOR THE BEETS

6 beets

2 tablespoons extra-virgin olive oil

1 tablespoon raw apple cider vinegar

FOR THE SALSA VERDE

1 avocado, peeled, pitted, and finely diced

1 jalapeño, seeded and minced

1 shallot, minced

1 bunch parsley, finely chopped

1 bunch cilantro, finely chopped

1 bunch chives, finely chopped

¼ cup extra-virgin olive oil

¼ cup raw apple cider vinegar

Himalayan salt

Freshly ground black pepper

This beautiful dish can be made even more striking if you use several different colors of beets. Just be sure to marinate them separately and assemble them only on the final dish, to prevent them from staining one another. You will have extra salsa verde left over, which can be saved for up to a day and used as a topping for raw noodles or on your favorite Buddha bowl.

TO MAKE THE BEETS

Peel the beets and slice them into very thin rounds with a mandoline. In a large bowl, whisk together the olive oil and cider vinegar. Add the beet rounds and let them marinate for 5 minutes.

TO MAKE THE SALSA VERDE

Combine all the ingredients in a bowl and toss gently with a spoon until the salsa comes together.

TO SERVE

Plate the beet rounds in concentric circles, slightly overlapping one another. Top with spoonfuls of salsa verde and serve.

DIY HACK: If you don't have a mandoline, cut each peeled beet in half, then place it cut-side down on a cutting board and slice it into thin half-moons.

cauliflower rice buddha bowls

NUT-FREE · UNDER 30 MINUTES

SERVES 2 · PREP: 10 MINUTES

1 cauliflower head, cut
    into florets

1 tablespoon tamari

1 tablespoon raw sesame oil

1 tablespoon grapeseed oil

1 teaspoon raw apple
    cider vinegar

1 teaspoon coconut sugar

2 teaspoons pickled ginger

1 carrot, peeled and
    julienned (see Prep Tip,
    page 153)

1 scallion, thinly sliced

1 avocado, peeled, pitted,
    and sliced

2 cups mung bean sprouts

½ cucumber, julienned (see
    Prep Tip, page 153)

Buddha bowls are my favorite way to use up leftovers and clean out my crisper drawer. In this Japanese-inspired bowl, the ingredients are tied together with a tangy-sweet mixture of sesame oil, tamari, cider vinegar, coconut sugar, and pickled ginger. Use it as a guide, and swap in whatever vegetables you like. The key is to start with a cauliflower rice base and top it with a good mix of fat, protein, fiber, and vitamins from different foods.

1. Work in batches to make the cauliflower rice. Put the cauliflower florets in the food processor, but fill the bowl only about two-thirds of the way. Pulse the cauliflower to the size of rice grains. As you pulse, some pieces may remain whole while others have already become rice. It's important to remove any big chunks and set aside the remaining rice as you go so that you don't end up with a paste. Continue with the rest of the florets. Then, at the end, return all the big chunks to the food processor and pulse so that you have processed the whole head of cauliflower. (If the core of the cauliflower is tender, you can use it as well.)

2. In a large bowl, whisk together the tamari, sesame oil, grapeseed oil, cider vinegar, and coconut sugar. Add the cauliflower rice and toss. Divide the rice between two bowls.

3. Top each bowl with portions of pickled ginger, carrot, scallion, avocado, mung bean sprouts, and cucumber and serve.

SUBSTITUTION: For an extra boost of protein and faux-fish flavor, add a dash of spirulina to this Buddha bowl. Spirulina is a powder made of algae, which is very popular for its nutrient profile. Not only is it high in protein, but it also contains healthy doses of antioxidants, B vitamins, and amino acids.

MARINATED CAULIFLOWER STEAKS
WITH CHIMICHURRI

CHAPTER 8

weekend entrées

raw lasagna

SOY-FREE

SERVES 2 · PREP: 40 MINUTES

FOR THE NOODLES

2 large zucchini

Pinch Himalayan salt

FOR THE "PARMESAN" TOPPING

¼ cup raw macadamia nuts

¼ cup nutritional yeast

Pinch Himalayan salt

FOR THE CASHEW BÉCHAMEL

½ cup raw cashews, soaked
for 8 hours and drained

2 to 3 tablespoons water

1 tablespoon extra-virgin
olive oil

1 tablespoon freshly
squeezed lemon juice

2 tablespoons
nutritional yeast

Himalayan salt

Freshly ground
black pepper

It takes a bit of effort to assemble all five elements of this lasagna, but trust me—it's well worth it. Take one bite of these long zucchini noodles with pesto and tomato sauces, creamy cashew béchamel, and macadamia "parmesan" topping, and you'll never look at raw food the same way again.

TO MAKE THE NOODLES

Cut off the ends of the zucchini and reserve for another recipe. Thinly slice the zucchini lengthwise, either by hand or with a mandoline. Set the slices on a kitchen towel and sprinkle with salt. Set aside while you make the sauces and topping.

TO MAKE THE "PARMESAN" TOPPING

In a blender or food processor, pulse the macadamia nuts to break them up until they have a sandy texture. Add the nutritional yeast and a pinch of salt. Set aside in a bowl and rinse out the blender.

TO MAKE THE CASHEW BÉCHAMEL

Combine the cashews, water, olive oil, and lemon juice in the blender and blend until a smooth cream forms, adding more water as needed. Add the nutritional yeast, season with salt and pepper, and blend just to combine. Set aside in a bowl and rinse out the blender.

FOR THE TOMATO SAUCE

2 beefsteak tomatoes or other meaty tomatoes, chopped

4 sun-dried tomatoes, drained and chopped

1 garlic clove, halved

1 tablespoon extra-virgin olive oil

Himalayan salt

Freshly ground black pepper

5 basil leaves, cut into chiffonade (see Prep Tip, page 96)

FOR THE PESTO

2 tablespoons raw pine nuts

1 garlic clove, halved

1 tablespoon nutritional yeast

1 cup basil leaves

¼ cup extra-virgin olive oil

Himalayan salt

Freshly ground black pepper

TO MAKE THE TOMATO SAUCE

Combine the fresh and sun-dried tomatoes in the blender and blend until smooth. Add the garlic and olive oil and blend until smooth. Season with salt and pepper. Transfer to a bowl. Stir the basil into the tomato sauce. Set aside and rinse out the blender.

TO MAKE THE PESTO

Combine the pine nuts, garlic, and nutritional yeast in the blender and pulse a few times to break up the garlic clove and pine nuts. Add the basil leaves and a drizzle of the olive oil. Blend on low speed, slowly drizzling in the remaining olive oil, until the pesto is smooth. Do not overblend, or you risk oxidizing the basil. Season the pesto with salt and pepper and set aside in a bowl.

TO ASSEMBLE THE LASAGNA

Spread a small base of the cashew béchamel on each plate, then top with one zucchini noodle. Top the noodle with a layer of béchamel, a layer of tomato sauce, and a layer of pesto. Add another noodle and continue. Depending on the thickness of your layers, you should be able to make 3 or 4 layers per plate. Top the final slice of zucchini with cashew béchamel, then sprinkle the macadamia "Parmesan" over the top. Serve immediately.

PREP TIP: Be sure not to stray from the recipe. If you make the sauces out of order, they may become discolored and will detract from the beauty of this dish.

raw quattro stagioni pizza

NUT-FREE · SOY-FREE

SERVES 2 · PREP: 40 MINUTES · DEHYDRATING: 5 HOURS

½ cup flax seeds, soaked for 10 minutes and drained

½ cup hemp hearts, soaked for 8 hours and drained

½ cup raw buckwheat groats, soaked for 8 hours and drained

1 red bell pepper, seeded and chopped

3 meaty heirloom tomatoes, 2 diced and 1 thinly sliced

2 sun-dried tomatoes, minced

1 garlic clove, minced

1 tablespoon nutritional yeast

2 button mushrooms, thinly sliced

1 kale leaf, torn into small pieces

¼ cup fresh peas

Each section of this "four seasons" pizza represents a time of year: tomatoes for summer, mushrooms for fall, kale for winter, and peas for spring. The crust, made of soaked seeds and grains, is soft and bready in texture, with a nutty flavor that complements any assortment of vegetables. Once you get the hang of this recipe, experiment with your favorite seasonal produce—the possibilities are endless.

1. Turn your oven to its lowest setting; if you have an oven thermometer, check to see that it doesn't go above 100°F. Line a baking sheet with parchment paper.

2. Combine the flax seeds, hemp hearts, buckwheat, and bell pepper in a blender or food processor and process until relatively smooth. Spread this mixture out in a circle on the lined baking sheet.

3. Place the crust in the oven and prop the door open so that it does not overheat. Dehydrate for 5 hours, then peel the crust from the baking sheet and set aside.

4. Combine the diced tomatoes, sun-dried tomatoes, and garlic in the blender and blend until smooth. Spread the sauce over the pizza crust.

5. Sprinkle the nutritional yeast over the sauce.

6. Arrange each of the four toppings—sliced tomatoes, mushrooms, kale, and peas—in one of the four quadrants of the pizza. Serve.

kelp noodle alfredo

SOY-FREE · UNDER 30 MINUTES

SERVES 2 · PREP: 25 MINUTES

2 cups kelp noodles, rinsed very well in warm water and drained

1 cup raw macadamia nuts, soaked for 8 hours and drained

½ cup raw pine nuts

¼ cup nutritional yeast

Juice of ½ lemon

½ cup water

2 tablespoons extra-virgin olive oil

1 garlic clove, minced

Freshly grated nutmeg

Himalayan salt

Freshly ground black pepper

Chopped fresh parsley, for garnish

If you're missing the rich, creamy comfort of Alfredo sauce, this pasta will fit the bill. While the macadamia nuts may be a bit expensive, this dish is totally worth it for a special occasion meal. If you've already hit your kelp noodle quota for the week, it's just as delicious on zucchini tagliatelle.

1. Put the kelp noodles in a bowl and set aside.

2. In a blender, combine the macadamia nuts, pine nuts, nutritional yeast, lemon juice, water, olive oil, garlic, nutmeg, season with salt and pepper, and blend until smooth.

3. Pour the sauce over the kelp noodles and toss to combine. Sprinkle some chopped parsley over the top and serve.

raw falafel with garlicky dipping sauce

NUT-FREE · SOY-FREE

SERVES 2 · PREP: 30 MINUTES · DEHYDRATING OR CHILLING: 5 HOURS

FOR THE FALAFEL

3 carrots, peeled and grated

1 cup sunflower
   seeds, chopped

1 cup sprouted chickpeas
   (see page 34)

1 shallot, minced

¼ cup chopped parsley

¼ cup raw tahini

Juice of ½ lemon

2 teaspoons ground
   coriander

2 teaspoons ground cumin

FOR THE GARLIC DIPPING SAUCE

¼ cup raw tahini

Juice of ½ lemon

1 tablespoon extra-virgin
   olive oil

2 garlic cloves, minced

You are faced with two options when it comes to these raw falafel. You can either chill them so that they hold together, and eat them straight out of the refrigerator, or you can dehydrate them in the oven to crisp them up a bit. Either way, they're positively delicious with the garlic dipping sauce.

TO MAKE THE FALAFEL

1. Combine all the falafel ingredients in a blender or food processor. Blend or process until the mixture is chunky but sticks together. Remove from the blender and roll into little balls.

2. The balls can either be dehydrated or chilled. To dehydrate without a dehydrator, turn your oven to its lowest setting; if you have an oven thermometer, check to see that it doesn't go above 100 degrees. Line a baking sheet with parchment paper and place the falafel balls on it. Put the baking sheet in the oven and prop the door open so that it does not overheat. Dehydrate the falafel for 5 hours, then remove from the oven.

3. If you'd rather chill them, place the falafel on a baking sheet and refrigerate until solid, 2 to 5 hours. »

raw falafel
with garlicky
dipping sauce

CONTINUED

TO MAKE THE GARLIC DIPPING SAUCE

1. Whisk together the tahini, lemon juice, olive oil, and garlic. Add water as needed until you get the consistency you want.

2. Serve the falafel with the dipping sauce.

pumpkin "soufflé"

SOY-FREE

SERVES 2 · PREP: 10 MINUTES · CHILLING: AT LEAST 5 HOURS

2 cups cubed pumpkin

1 garlic clove, minced

1 cup unsweetened
    hazelnut milk,
    homemade (see page 79)
    or store-bought

2 tablespoons chia seeds

½ teaspoon flax seeds

1 fresh sage leaf, chopped

Freshly grated nutmeg

Himalayan salt

Freshly ground
    black pepper

Thanks to the addition of chia seeds, these savory treats can hold their own on a plate. Pair them with kale salad for a satisfying autumnal meal, or enjoy them on their own as a midday snack.

Combine all the ingredients in a blender or food processor and blend until smooth. Pour the mixture into ramekins and refrigerate until set, 5 to 12 hours.

SUBSTITUTION: This recipe also works well with sweet potato or a mix of pumpkin and sweet potato.

marinated cauliflower steaks with chimichurri

NUT-FREE · SOY-FREE · UNDER $10 · UNDER 30 MINUTES

SERVES 2 · PREP: 25 MINUTES

¼ cup plus 1 tablespoon extra-virgin olive oil, divided

Juice of 1 lemon

4 (1-inch-thick) cauliflower steaks, cut from the center of a head of cauliflower

¼ cup raw apple cider vinegar

1 tablespoon agave nectar

1 bunch parsley, finely chopped

1 bunch cilantro, finely chopped

1 bunch scallions, finely chopped

Cauliflower can be a great stand-in for steak when topped with a chimichurri sauce. While the steaks are marinating, take the time to finely chop all the herbs for the sauce. The more finely you chop them, the more pleasant the mouthfeel of the sauce will be. You'll end up with extra chimichurri, which can be used as a dip or added to your favorite Buddha bowl recipe.

1. In a shallow dish, whisk together 1 tablespoon of olive oil and the lemon juice. Add the cauliflower steaks and turn them to coat well. Set aside to marinate for 10 minutes.

2. In a small bowl, combine the remaining ¼ cup of olive oil, cider vinegar, agave, parsley, cilantro, and scallions and mix well.

3. Plate the steaks and serve topped with dollops of chimichurri sauce.

PLAN AHEAD: Save any pieces of cauliflower that are discarded when cutting the steaks and use them to make cauliflower rice.

vegetable noodles with puttanesca sauce

NUT-FREE · SOY-FREE · UNDER $10 · UNDER 30 MINUTES

SERVES 2 · PREP: 25 MINUTES

1 zucchini, cut into ribbons with a vegetable peeler

1 carrot, peeled and cut into ribbons with a vegetable peeler

4 meaty heirloom tomatoes, diced

1 shallot, minced

1 garlic clove, minced

¼ cup black or brown olives, pitted and halved

2 sun-dried tomatoes, minced

1 tablespoon capers, minced

4 basil leaves, cut into chiffonade (see Prep Tip, page 96)

1 tablespoon extra-virgin olive oil

Puttanesca sauce is said to have been invented in Italy based on whatever ingredients were lying around after all of the *puttas,* or prostitutes, finished work for the night. Regardless of how it was invented, it's positively delicious, with a unique briny flavor. In this version, a raw puttanesca sauce is used as a topping for vegetable noodles.

1. In a large bowl, combine the zucchini and carrot ribbons.

2. In another bowl, combine the diced tomatoes, shallot, and garlic and mix, crushing the tomatoes a bit with a spoon. Add the olives, sun-dried tomatoes, capers, basil, and olive oil and mix well.

3. Toss the sauce with the pasta and serve.

PREP TIP: For a special presentation, use a pastry ring or a can with both the top and bottom cut out, and pack the pasta into the ring on a plate. Remove the ring, and the pasta should stand on its own. If your pasta sauce is a bit watery, strain the pasta and the sauce a bit before attempting this plating trick.

zucchini rollatini

SOY-FREE

SERVES 2 · PREP: 40 MINUTES

FOR THE
CASHEW FILLING

1 cup raw cashews, soaked
for 8 hours and drained

5 to 6 tablespoons water

2 tablespoons extra-virgin
olive oil

2 tablespoons freshly
squeezed lemon juice

4 tablespoons
nutritional yeast

Himalayan salt

Freshly ground
black pepper

5 basil leaves, cut into
chiffonade (see Prep Tip,
page 96)

FOR THE TOMATO SAUCE

4 meaty heirloom
tomatoes, diced

1 garlic clove, minced

1 tablespoon extra-virgin
olive oil

Himalayan salt

Freshly ground
black pepper

FOR THE ROLLATINI

2 zucchini, thinly sliced
lengthwise and spread
out on a dishtowel

Chopped fresh parsley,
for garnish

Chopped raw macadamia
nuts, for garnish

1 tablespoon
nutritional yeast

Zucchini and eggplant rollatini are classics of Italian-American cuisine. This raw version is a fun play on the traditional recipes, a bit like a rolled raw lasagna. Cut the zucchini as thinly as you can in order to make rolling easier. If you can make this dish a bit in advance, resting the zucchini will allow the rollatini to hold together better as they're served.

TO MAKE THE CASHEW FILLING

1. Combine the cashews, water, olive oil, and lemon juice in a blender and blend until a smooth cream forms.

2. Add the nutritional yeast, season with salt and pepper, and blend just to combine. Fold in the basil. Transfer to a bowl and set aside. »

zucchini rollatini

CONTINUED

TO MAKE THE TOMATO SAUCE

1. In a bowl, combine the tomatoes, garlic, and olive oil and toss to combine.

2. Season with salt and pepper.

TO MAKE THE ROLLATINI

1. Place a heaping tablespoon of cashew filling on the end of a zucchini slice and carefully roll it up. Place the rollatini, seam-side down, in a casserole dish. Continue until you have rolled all the zucchini or used all the filling.

2. Top the entire dish with the tomato sauce, then sprinkle the parsley, chopped macadamia nuts, and nutritional yeast over the top. Serve.

raw paella

NUT-FREE · SOY-FREE · UNDER $10

SERVES 2 · PREP: 40 MINUTES

1 cauliflower head, cut
  into florets

Juice of 1 lemon

1 tablespoon
  nutritional yeast

2 teaspoons ground
  turmeric

2 teaspoons paprika

1 zucchini, finely diced

1 yellow summer squash,
  finely diced

2 tomatoes, diced

½ cup green peas

1 red bell pepper, seeded
  and diced

½ bunch parsley, chopped

3 tablespoons extra-virgin
  olive oil

The cauliflower rice is tinged yellow with turmeric and paprika in this raw paella, and a variety of vegetables adds bursts of color and tons of nutrients.

1. Work in batches to make the cauliflower rice. Put the cauliflower florets in the food processor, but fill the bowl only about two-thirds of the way. Pulse the cauliflower to the size of rice grains. As you pulse, some pieces may remain whole while others have already become rice. It's important to remove any big chunks and set aside the remaining rice as you go so that you don't end up with a paste. Continue with the rest of the florets. Then, at the end, return all the big chunks to the food processor and pulse so that you have processed the whole head of cauliflower. (If the core of the cauliflower is tender, you can use it as well.)

2. In a small bowl, combine the lemon juice, nutritional yeast, turmeric, and paprika. Whisk until the spices have dissolved.

3. Pat the cauliflower rice dry with paper towels or a kitchen towel and transfer to a large bowl. Add the spiced lemon juice, tossing to make sure that the cauliflower is well coated. It should take on a yellowish hue.

4. Add the zucchini, squash, tomatoes, peas, bell pepper, parsley, and olive oil and toss to combine. Serve.

SUBSTITUTION: If you prefer, you could also use saffron to flavor and color the cauliflower rice.

raw chili

4 button mushrooms, finely diced

2 tablespoons raw apple cider vinegar

2 tomatoes, diced, divided

1 avocado, peeled, pitted, and cubed

2 dates, chopped

1 garlic clove, minced

¾ cup sun-dried tomatoes, finely chopped

⅓ cup raw cashews, soaked for 8 hours and drained

⅓ cup raw walnuts, soaked for 8 hours and drained

1 tablespoon tamari

1 cup sprouted adzuki beans (see page 34)

2 scallions, thinly sliced

1 red bell pepper, seeded and finely diced

1 carrot, peeled and finely diced

1 tablespoon chili powder

Himalayan salt

Freshly ground black pepper

Who says you can't have a delicious, filling bowl of chili while on a raw food diet? This version is bursting with umami flavor thanks to the sprouted adzuki beans and nut-based sauce. Try to chop all your vegetables evenly for a beautiful plate, and feel free to top it with Habanero Hot Sauce (page 203).

1. In a bowl, toss the mushrooms with the cider vinegar. Set aside to marinate for 20 minutes.

2. Combine half of the diced tomatoes, the avocado, dates, garlic, sun-dried tomatoes, cashews, walnuts, and tamari in a blender. Blend until fairly smooth. Pour into a bowl.

3. Drain the mushrooms of any excess liquid and add them to the bowl, along with the remaining diced tomato, the adzuki beans, scallions, bell pepper, carrot, and chili powder. Toss to combine. Season with salt and pepper and serve.

DIY HACK: You can make your own chili powder by combining equal parts dried oregano, ground cumin, garlic granules, and cayenne pepper, and matching this quantity of spice with an equal quantity of paprika.

kale summer rolls
with satay dipping sauce

SERVES 2 · PREP: 1 HOUR

FOR THE KALE WRAPS

6 large kale leaves

2 tablespoons tamari

1 tablespoon raw apple
cider vinegar

FOR THE SATAY SAUCE

1 cup raw cashews, soaked
for 8 hours and drained

1 (14-ounce) can
coconut milk

Juice of ½ lime

1 tablespoon tamari

2 teaspoons coconut sugar

½ small onion, grated

1 garlic clove, minced

1 Thai chile, seeded
and minced

FOR THE SUMMER ROLLS

1 avocado, peeled, pitted,
and sliced

2 carrots, peeled and
julienned (see Prep Tip)

1 red bell pepper, seeded
and julienned (see
Prep Tip)

1 yellow bell pepper, seeded
and julienned (see
Prep Tip)

1 cup mung bean sprouts

¼ cup chopped fresh cilantro

Summer rolls are a beautiful way to serve up a whole lot of different vegetables, and despite their name, these rolls can be made all year long. They're particularly delicious stuffed with cabbage ferments like kimchi or sauerkraut, or any sprouted bean or lentil.

TO MAKE THE KALE WRAPS

1. Lay out the kale leaves flat and carefully cut away any large stems. Be sure that the leaf remains mostly whole, as it is going to be the wrap for the rolls, and any holes could be problematic.

2. Combine the tamari and cider vinegar in a dish and add the kale leaves, making sure to coat each one. Marinate for about 10 minutes while you prepare the satay sauce.

TO MAKE THE SATAY SAUCE

1. Combine all the satay sauce ingredients in a blender. Blend until relatively smooth, taking care not to over-heat the sauce.

2. Divide the satay sauce between two small ramekins. »

kale summer rolls with satay dipping sauce

CONTINUED

TO MAKE THE SUMMER ROLLS

1. Remove the kale leaves from the marinade and pat dry with paper towels. Place each kale leaf flat on the work surface with the long side facing you. Arrange a portion of each of the vegetables in a pile on the upper right side of the kale leaf, perpendicular to the kale leaf itself. Fold the bottom portion of the kale leaf up to cover the vegetables, then roll the kale leaf from right to left, bunching the vegetables together and slowly wrapping them in the leaf. Secure by placing the seam-side down on the plate or by using toothpicks, if needed.

2. Serve 3 summer rolls per person, with a ramekin of sauce on each plate.

PREP TIP: Julienne is a cutting style that leaves you with thin sticks of vegetables. To julienne, first cut your vegetable into sections about 4 inches long, then cut the sections into lengthwise slices. Cut these slices into matchsticks that are all the same width.

CHAPTER 9

sides
& snacks

savory cucumber ants-on-a-log with cashew "cheese" and goji berries

SOY-FREE · UNDER $10 · UNDER 30 MINUTES

SERVES 2 · PREP: 10 MINUTES

1 cucumber, halved
   lengthwise

½ cup raw cashews, soaked
   for 8 hours and drained

2 to 3 tablespoons water

1 tablespoon extra-virgin
   olive oil

1 tablespoon freshly
   squeezed lemon juice

2 tablespoons
   nutritional yeast

Himalayan salt

Freshly ground
   black pepper

¼ cup goji berries

For a quick snack, top cucumber boats with a raw cashew "cheese" filling and superfruit goji berries. Long consumed in Asia for their health benefits, these tart berries add just the right amount of color and a light hint of sweetness to this savory snack.

1. Scrape the seeds out of each cucumber half with a spoon. Cut the cucumbers into sections about 3 inches long.

2. In a blender, combine the cashews, water, olive oil, lemon juice, nutritional yeast, season with salt and pepper, and blend until smooth.

3. Fill the cucumber boats with the cashew "cheese," then top with goji berries. Serve.

kale chips

NUT-FREE · SOY-FREE · UNDER $10

SERVES 2 · PREP: 10 MINUTES · DEHYDRATING: 10 HOURS

1 head kale, torn into
   bite-size pieces

1 tablespoon extra-virgin
   olive oil

1 teaspoon Himalayan salt

When dehydrated, kale becomes crispy and crunchy, all the while retaining its earthy flavor. And with the addition of some olive oil and a sprinkling of salt, these chips are downright addictive.

1. Put the kale in a bowl and add the olive oil. Massage the oil into the kale with your fingers until the kale is soft, about 45 seconds.

2. Turn your oven to its lowest setting; if you have an oven temperature, check to see that it doesn't go above 100 degrees. Place a rack over a baking sheet.

3. Spread out the kale on the rack in an even layer, and sprinkle with the salt. Place the kale in the oven and prop the door open so that it does not overheat. Dehydrate until the kale is crisp, about 10 hours.

PREP TIP: The kale chips can also be made in a dehydrator if you have one.

marinated stuffed mushroom caps

SOY-FREE

MAKES 10 CAPS · PREP: 10 MINUTES · DRAINING AND MARINATING: 1 HOUR

FOR THE MUSHROOMS

10 cremini or button
  mushroom caps

1 tablespoon Himalayan
  salt, plus more for
  seasoning

½ cup extra-virgin olive oil

Grated zest and juice
  of 1 lemon

Freshly ground
  black pepper

1 garlic clove, minced

FOR THE PESTO

4 tablespoons raw pine nuts

2 tablespoons
  nutritional yeast

1 garlic clove, halved

2 cups fresh basil leaves

¼ cup extra-virgin olive oil

Himalayan salt

Freshly ground
  black pepper

Even though you've probably been eating raw mushrooms your whole life, it isn't the best of ideas. Not only are mushrooms difficult to digest raw, but some contain irritating or toxic components that are broken down with cooking. That doesn't mean that mushrooms can't be part of your raw diet; it just means that you have to "cook" them in a marinade first.

TO MAKE THE MUSHROOMS

1. Place the mushrooms in a colander and toss with the salt. Allow to sit for 30 minutes so that the excess water is drawn out of the mushrooms.

2. Whisk together the olive oil, lemon zest and juice, and season with salt and pepper. Add the garlic. When the mushrooms have drained for 30 minutes, pat them dry and add them to the bowl of marinade. Marinate for 30 minutes.

TO MAKE THE PESTO

1. Combine the pine nuts, nutritional yeast, and garlic in a blender and pulse a few times to break up the garlic clove and pine nuts. Add the basil leaves and a drizzle of the olive oil. Blend on low speed, slowly drizzling in the remaining olive oil, until the pesto is smooth. Do not overblend, or you risk oxidizing the basil. Season the pesto with salt and pepper.

2. Fill each mushroom cap with pesto. Serve immediately.

broccoli with "cheesy" sauce

SOY-FREE · UNDER $10 · UNDER 30 MINUTES

SERVES 2 · PREP: 10 MINUTES · MARINATING: 20 MINUTES

1 head broccoli, cut
    into florets

Juice of 1 lemon

2 cups raw cashews, soaked
    for 8 hours and drained

1 red bell pepper, seeded
    and roughly chopped

½ to 1 cup water

¾ cup nutritional yeast

2 tablespoons raw apple
    cider vinegar

1 garlic clove, halved

2 teaspoons ground
    turmeric

Himalayan salt

Freshly ground
    black pepper

This raw version of a comfort food favorite is great as a side dish or snack. The raw broccoli is marinated in lemon juice to help make it a bit easier to digest. You can either serve the "cheese" sauce on the side for dipping or drizzle it over the top. The combination of broccoli and red bell pepper makes this snack a vitamin C powerhouse.

1. Put the broccoli in a bowl and squeeze the lemon juice over it. Toss to coat and set aside to marinate for 20 minutes.

2. Meanwhile, make the "cheese" sauce. Combine the cashews and bell pepper in a blender and add a bit of water to help them blend. Purée until a paste forms. Add the nutritional yeast, cider vinegar, garlic, and turmeric and continue to blend until smooth, adding more water as needed until you get a creamy consistency. Season with salt and pepper.

3. Serve the "cheese" sauce over the broccoli or on the side.

spicy stuffed avocado halves

NUT-FREE · SOY-FREE · UNDER $10 · UNDER 30 MINUTES

SERVES 2 · PREP: 10 MINUTES

1 button mushroom

Juice and zest of
1 lemon, divided

½ tomato, finely diced

1 shallot, minced

½ poblano pepper, seeded
and finely diced

¼ jalapeño, seeded
and minced

1 avocado, halved
and pitted

Himalayan salt

2 tablespoons raw
sunflower seeds

2 tablespoons mung
bean sprouts

Fresh herbs, for garnish

Stuffed avocados are easy to prepare and delicious, especially when seasoned with tomato, chiles, and lime. And thanks to their high fat content, they are one of the most filling snacks available on a raw diet.

1. Thinly slice the mushroom and top with a bit of lemon juice. Allow to marinate about 10 minutes, while you prepare the other ingredients.

2. In a small bowl, combine the tomato, shallot, pepper, jalapeño, and mushroom slices. Squeeze the remaining lime juice over the avocado halves, then fill with the spicy salsa and top with a pinch of salt, a scattering of sunflower seeds, mung bean sprouts, lemon zest, and whatever fresh herbs you like. Serve immediately.

SUBSTITUTION: You can also fill your avocados with your favorite salsa or one of the sauces from chapter 12.

"goat cheese" log

SOY-FREE · UNDER $10

SERVES 2 · PREP: 40 MINUTES · CHILLING: 30–60 MINUTES

½ cup raw cashews, soaked for 8 hours and drained

Juice of ½ lemon

⅓ cup water

1 tablespoon coconut oil

1 teaspoon raw apple cider vinegar

Pinch Himalayan salt

2 tablespoons herbes de Provence

The tang of true goat cheese really comes through in this spread. It's fantastic served with raw flatbread and apple slices or crumbled onto your favorite salad. Don't skip the chilling step; it's essential to give this "goat cheese" its texture.

1. Combine the cashews, lemon juice, water, coconut oil, cider vinegar, and salt in a blender. Blend until smooth, adding more water if necessary.

2. Place a sheet of plastic wrap on your work surface. Arrange the cashew mixture in a log shape on the plastic wrap, and roll it up to make it even. Depending on how solid your "cheese" is, you may or may not need to chill it for 30 minutes at this point. Unroll.

3. Scatter the herbes de Provence over a new sheet of plastic wrap, and transfer the log to the new sheet. Roll the "cheese" log in the herbes de Provence until evenly coated, then wrap in the new sheet of plastic wrap and chill for 30 minutes more. Unwrap to serve.

sweet banana ants-on-a-log with cinnamon nut butter and cacao nibs

SOY-FREE · UNDER 30 MINUTES

SERVES 2 · PREP: 10 MINUTES

1 cup raw cashews, soaked for 8 hours and drained

1 cup raw almonds, soaked for 8 hours and drained

1 teaspoon ground cinnamon

½ teaspoon Himalayan salt

1 to 2 tablespoons unsweetened cashew or almond milk, homemade (see page 79) or store-bought

2 bananas, halved lengthwise

¼ cup cacao nibs

Who didn't love ants-on-a-log as a child? This version uses cinnamon-scented cashew-almond butter in place of the more traditional peanut butter. You'll end up with more nut butter than you need, but keep it on hand for snack emergencies.

1. Combine the cashews, almonds, cinnamon, and salt in a blender or food processor and blend until smooth, adding a bit of nut milk as needed to keep the blender going. This will be far easier in a food processor; in a blender, you may have to stop the motor a few times to keep it from overheating.

2. Spread some nut butter over the banana halves and top with cacao nibs. Serve.

SUBSTITUTION: Use raisins in place of cacao nibs.

apple slices with raw honey and cashew "cheese"

SOY-FREE · UNDER $10 · UNDER 30 MINUTES

SERVES 4 · PREP: 10 MINUTES

2 cups raw cashews, soaked for 8 hours and drained

1 red bell pepper, seeded and roughly chopped

1 garlic clove, halved

¾ cup nutritional yeast

2 tablespoons raw apple cider vinegar

2 teaspoons ground turmeric

Himalayan salt

Freshly ground black pepper

2 green apples, cored and sliced

2 red apples, cored and sliced

¼ cup raw honey

Do you miss having a cheese platter as an appetizer, dessert, or snack? This raw version combines cashew "cheese" with apple slices and a touch of raw honey for a snack that hits both your protein and carb needs for an afternoon pick-me-up.

1. Combine the cashews, bell pepper, garlic, nutritional yeast, cider vinegar, and turmeric in a blender or food processor. Blend, scraping down the sides of the blender as needed, until you get a smooth "cheese." You may have to stop and start your blender to keep it from overheating. If you have a food processor, this process will go more quickly. Season with salt and pepper.

2. Put servings of the "cheese" in individual ramekins, and place the apples on plates. Drizzle honey over the apples and serve.

SUBSTITUTION: You could also serve these "cheese" plates with grapes, raw crackers, or even kale chips.

almond butter–stuffed dates

SOY-FREE · UNDER 30 MINUTES

SERVES 2 · PREP: 10 MINUTES

1 cup raw almonds, soaked
  for 8 hours and drained
1 tablespoon coconut oil
½ teaspoon Himalayan salt
1 to 2 tablespoons Raw
  Almond Milk (page 76)
30 whole dates

These sweet morsels are super addictive. They're a great snack idea for the afternoon, thanks to the balance of protein from the nuts and sugar from the dates. You can prepare them in advance and keep them in the refrigerator for when hunger strikes, but honestly, they're so quick to put together that you have no excuse not to make them the moment you want them.

1. Combine the almonds, coconut oil, and salt in a blender or food processor. Blend until fairly smooth, adding almond milk as needed to help the blades turn. Do not thin out the almond butter too much, or it won't hold when you're stuffing the dates.

2. Slice the dates lengthwise, just on one side. Remove the pit, keeping the opposite side of the date intact. Stuff each date with about a teaspoon of almond butter. Serve.

PLAN AHEAD: Having this nut butter in the refrigerator means that you're never far from snack heaven!

on-the-go energy bites

SOY-FREE · UNDER 30 MINUTES

MAKES 16 · PREP: 10 MINUTES

⅓ cup raw buckwheat
  groats, soaked for 8
  hours and drained

⅓ cup almonds, soaked for
  8 hours and drained

⅓ cup hemp hearts, soaked
  for 8 hours and drained

¼ cup cacao nibs

1 cup dates, pitted
  and chopped

½ cup raw dried apricots,
  pitted and chopped

Sweetened with raw dates and packed with protein and vital nutrients, these energy bites are perfect for a midday pick-me-up or grab-and-go breakfast. Make a big batch over the weekend and store them in the refrigerator for when hunger strikes.

1. Combine all the ingredients in a blender or food processor. If you are using a blender, be aware that your energy bites may be a bit chunkier and you may have to start and stop your blender a few times to finish blending. Add water as needed to help the mixture come together.

2. When the mixture sticks together, place it in a bowl and roll it into bites. Your energy bites are ready! Keep them in the refrigerator.

SUBSTITUTION: You can coat your energy bites in cocoa powder, unsweetened shredded coconut, cocoa nibs, a mix of cinnamon and coconut sugar, or ground flax seeds, if you like.

CABBAGE, APPLE, AND
CARROT KIMCHI

refrigerator half-sour pickles

NUT-FREE · SOY-FREE · UNDER $10

MAKES 1 QUART · PREP: 10 MINUTES · FERMENTING: 2 DAYS

9 small Kirby cucumbers, blossom ends trimmed

2 cups raw apple cider vinegar

1 cup filtered water

1 tablespoon kosher salt

½ bunch dill

5 garlic cloves, peeled

2 tablespoons coriander seeds

Pickles are a super tasty snack to have on hand. The only thing to bear in mind is that because you won't be adding boiling water to the jar, you want to make sure that both the jar and the pickles are very clean, and that goes for any ferment you're making. Run the jar through a hot cycle in the dishwasher, and be sure to scrub the cucumbers well.

1. Cut each cucumber lengthwise into four spears.

2. Combine the vinegar, water, and salt in a pot or bowl. Stir until the salt dissolves into the liquid.

3. Put the dill, garlic cloves, and coriander seeds in a quart-size mason jar, then pack the cucumber spears into the jar on top of the seasoning. Pour the pickling liquid over the cucumbers until the jar is completely full. Close the jar.

4. Place the jar in the refrigerator and chill for 2 days before serving. Your pickles will continue to get stronger in flavor the longer you keep them.

pickled watermelon rind

NUT-FREE · SOY-FREE · UNDER $10

MAKES 1 QUART · PREP: 10 MINUTES · FERMENTING: 2 DAYS

1 quart water

2 tablespoons kosher salt

Rind from 1 watermelon, all pink flesh and green skin removed, cut into 1-inch squares

1 tablespoon whole cloves

1 tablespoon whole black peppercorns

Waste not, want not! That's the theory behind watermelon rind pickles, which are delicious to boot. Toss them into your next summer salad or Buddha bowl. If you like them on the sweeter side, add a tablespoon of agave to the brine.

1. Combine the water and salt in a pot or bowl. Stir until the salt dissolves.

2. Put the watermelon rind, cloves, and peppercorns in a large jar. Weigh down the watermelon rind with another smaller jar filled with weights so that it will remain submerged. Fill the jar to the top with the salted water. Cover with a cloth, secured with a rubber band to the mouth of the jar.

3. Culture at room temperature for about 2 days, checking on the pickles daily. When the desired texture and flavor are achieved, store in the refrigerator.

sauerkraut

NUT-FREE · SOY-FREE · UNDER $10

MAKES 1 QUART · PREP: 10 MINUTES · FERMENTING: AT LEAST 2 DAYS

1 medium head green
cabbage, thinly sliced
1½ tablespoons kosher salt
1 tablespoon caraway seeds

It's a good idea to always have a batch of sauerkraut brewing so that you can toss some into your lettuce or kale wraps or onto a Buddha bowl, or just eat as is. This version includes caraway seeds, which are traditional, but you can also make plain sauerkraut if you want it to be more versatile for different types of dishes.

1. Put the cabbage and salt in a bowl. Massage the salt into the cabbage with your fingers until the cabbage is wet, 10 to 15 minutes. Add the caraway seeds.

2. Pack the cabbage into a large jar and add any juices that have been released. Weigh down the cabbage with another smaller jar filled with weights. Cover with a cloth, secured with a rubber band to the mouth of the jar. Press down on the cabbage every few hours so that it remains fully submerged in liquid, then ferment at room temperature for 2 to 10 days. When the desired texture and flavor are achieved, store in the refrigerator.

curtido

MAKES 1 QUART

PREP: 15 MINUTES · RESTING: 1 HOUR · FERMENTATION: 2 DAYS

1 small head cabbage
   (about 2 pounds), cored
   and shredded

2 carrots, shredded

½ red onion, shredded

4 green onions, thinly sliced

Small handful
   cilantro, minced

2 serrano chiles, minced

1 teaspoon red
   pepper flakes

1 teaspoon pickling salt

¼ cup white wine vinegar

2 tablespoons
   pineapple juice

The lightly fermented *curtido* hails from El Salvador and is similar to coleslaw. Shredded cabbage, carrots, onions, and chiles come together to create the mildly spicy and distinctive flavor of this classic dish. Fermented for a couple of days—which is quick compared with the much longer time needed to create sauerkraut—curtido retains a crisp texture and crunchiness that set it apart from other cabbage-based concoctions.

1. Mix the cabbage, carrots, red onion, green onions, cilantro, and chiles in a nonreactive bowl and add the red pepper flakes and salt.

2. Leave the vegetables sitting at room temperature for about 1 hour, or until they release some liquid.

3. Pack the vegetables into a quart jar, and press them down with a clean hand to remove air pockets. Pour the brine from the bowl into the jar, and add the white wine vinegar and pineapple juice. Press the vegetables down so that they are completely covered by the brine.

4. Use a weight to hold the cabbage and other vegetables below the surface.

5. Place a lid loosely on the jar and leave it at room temperature for 2 days.

6. Close the lid tightly. Transfer the curtido to the refrigerator, where it can be stored for up to 3 weeks.

kimchi

NUT-FREE · SOY-FREE · UNDER $10

MAKES 1 QUART · PREP: 10 MINUTES · FERMENTING: AT LEAST 1 DAY

1 napa cabbage head, halved lengthwise and thinly sliced crosswise

1½ tablespoons kosher salt

5 garlic cloves, minced

1 (½-inch) piece ginger, peeled and grated

1 teaspoon coconut sugar

3 tablespoons Korean red pepper flakes

4 scallions, thinly sliced

1 bunch chives, chopped

4 carrots, julienned (see Prep Tip, page 153)

Kimchi is a traditional Korean lacto-ferment that's delicious in all sorts of Asian-inspired dishes. I love putting some on my cauliflower "fried" rice or Buddha bowls, but it's also delicious on its own. You can play with the size of the cabbage pieces for different textures; traditionally, the cabbage pieces are left quite a bit larger than in sauerkraut, but these will take longer to ferment entirely.

1. Put the cabbage and salt in a bowl. Massage the salt into the cabbage with your fingers until the cabbage is wet, 10 to 15 minutes.

2. Combine the garlic, ginger, coconut sugar, and red pepper flakes in a bowl to make a paste.

3. Toss together the spice paste, scallions, chives, and carrots. Mix until well combined. Add the cabbage and mix to combine.

4. Pack the mixture into a jar, adding any liquid that the cabbage has released. Weigh down the cabbage with another smaller jar filled with weights. Cover with a cloth, secured with a rubber band to the mouth of the jar. Press down on the cabbage every few hours so that it remains submerged in liquid, then ferment for 1 to 5 days at room temperature. When the desired texture and flavor are achieved, store in the refrigerator.

radish kimchi

NUT-FREE · UNDER $10

MAKES 1 QUART · PREP: 10 MINUTES · FERMENTING: AT LEAST 1 DAY

6 cups filtered water

2 teaspoons kosher salt

½ teaspoon tamari

12 ounces yellow radishes, thinly sliced into rounds

1 small onion, thinly sliced

2 garlic cloves, thinly sliced

1 (½-inch) piece fresh ginger, peeled and grated

3 tablespoons Korean red pepper flakes

This kimchi is a bit different than the cabbage version, but no less delicious. Be sure to use filtered water; regular tap water might interfere with the ferment. It's a bit milder in flavor, and the radishes have a natural sweetness that make them the perfect topping for Buddha bowls.

1. Put the water, salt, and tamari in a bowl and stir until the salt dissolves.

2. Combine the radishes, onion, garlic, ginger, and red pepper flakes in another bowl and mix well to combine. Pack into a quart-size jar. Weigh down the radishes with another smaller jar filled with weights. Pour in the seasoned water.

3. Cover with a cloth, secured with a rubber band to the mouth of the jar. Ferment for 1 to 2 days at room temperature. When the desired texture and flavor are achieved, store in the refrigerator.

cabbage, apple, and carrot kimchi

MAKES 1 QUART

PREP: 20 MINUTES · RESTING: 4 TO 6 HOURS · FERMENTATION: 3 TO 6 DAYS

1 small head Chinese
cabbage (about
1½ pounds)

2 tablespoons plus 1
teaspoon pickling
salt, divided

2 carrots, grated

1 small crisp apple, grated

2 scallions, thinly sliced

1 teaspoon ginger, minced

1 garlic clove

¾ teaspoon Korean ground
hot pepper

1 cup water

Carrot adds crunch and apple brings a hint of sweetness to this alternative kimchi, a tasty twist on tradition. There are as many ways to make kimchi as the imagination allows, and this is a Japanese-inspired one. This slightly sweet kimchi can be eaten along with cauliflower rice for a light meal.

1. Cut the Chinese cabbage into 2-inch squares. Place the cabbage in a nonreactive bowl, and sprinkle it with 2 tablespoons of pickling salt; mix well so that the pieces are evenly covered. Place a clean kitchen towel on top, and leave the mixture to sit at room temperature for several hours, until it is reduced in size by at least half. Drain the excess water from the bowl. Fill the bowl with water, and rinse the cabbage again, pressing it to remove as much water as possible.

2. Mix all the remaining ingredients, including the additional teaspoon of pickling salt. Pack into a quart jar, and top the jar with water.

3. Place a lid or a top with an air lock on the jar, and leave the jar in a cool area of your kitchen for 3 to 6 days. If using a standard top, loosen the cap daily after fermentation begins, to allow gas to escape.

4. Once the kimchi is fermented to your liking, cap the jar tightly and store it in the refrigerator.

moroccan preserved lemons

NUT-FREE · SOY-FREE · UNDER $10

MAKES 1 QUART · PREP: 10 MINUTES · FERMENTING: 2 DAYS

5 Meyer lemons

8 teaspoons kosher
  salt, divided

Juice of 1 regular lemon

1 teaspoon cumin seeds

1 teaspoon coriander seeds

2 bay leaves

Filtered water

If you've never had preserved lemons, you might find them surprising. Unlike other lemons, the pulp or flesh is not used; it's the peel that's a coveted flavoring for all sorts of traditional Moroccan dishes. They go great as a garnish or ingredient in Raw Falafel with Garlicky Dipping Sauce (page 141), or you can use them as a seasoning on your Buddha bowls. You can also chop them finely and add them to your favorite salad dressing for an extra burst of flavor.

1. Remove the end of each Meyer lemon, then quarter them down toward the end without slicing clear through; each lemon will be sectioned but still hold together.

2. Put 1 teaspoon of salt in the bottom of a 1-quart mason jar. Put 1 teaspoon of salt into each Meyer lemon. Place 1 lemon in the jar, cut side down, pressing so that some of the juice is released into the jar. Add 1 teaspoon of salt, then the next lemon, then another 1 teaspoon of salt, and then the last lemon. Top with the last 1 teaspoon of salt. Squeeze the juice from the regular lemon over the Meyer lemons. Add the cumin seeds, coriander seeds, and bay leaves.

3. Weigh down the lemons with another smaller jar filled with weights so that it remains submerged. Fill the jar to the top with filtered water if the lemon juice isn't already covering them. Cover with a cloth, secured with a rubber band to the mouth of the jar. Ferment for 2 to 3 days at room temperature. After 3 days, close the jar with a lid and shake to disperse the flavors. Store in the refrigerator.

CACAO NIB
TRUFFLES

CHAPTER 11

desserts

balsamic strawberries with coconut whipped cream

NUT-FREE · SOY-FREE

SERVES 2 · PREP: 15 MINUTES · FREEZING: 1 HOUR

½ cup chopped fresh coconut meat, from 1 young Thai coconut

1 tablespoon coconut oil

2 tablespoons coconut sugar, divided

2 cups quartered fresh strawberries

1 tablespoon balsamic vinegar

These marinated strawberries have a pleasingly pungent flavor thanks to the balsamic vinegar. Topped with a raw vegan whipped cream, they're positively delicious! You should know that the jury's still out on balsamic vinegar; it's not technically raw, so you won't want to be using it that often. That said, given that you're going for a "mostly raw" diet, it's your call as to whether you'd like to use it. If not, you could always drizzle some lemon juice over the berries instead.

1. Combine the coconut meat, coconut oil, and 1 tablespoon of coconut sugar in a blender and blend until smooth, with a whipped-cream consistency. Transfer to a container and freeze for 1 hour.

2. Meanwhile, toss the strawberries with the balsamic vinegar and remaining 1 tablespoon of coconut sugar. Serve the strawberries with a dollop of chilled coconut cream on top.

PLAN AHEAD: Make the coconut cream in advance and store it in the coldest part of your refrigerator; this will allow it to keep its texture without fully freezing and being impossible to scoop.

raw chocolate-avocado pudding

SOY-FREE · UNDER $10 · UNDER 30 MINUTES

SERVES 2 · PREP: 5 MINUTES

1 avocado, peeled, pitted, and cubed

¼ cup unsweetened cocoa powder

3 tablespoons unsweetened nut milk, homemade (see page 79) or store-bought

3 tablespoons date paste

This is one of the easiest raw vegan desserts you'll ever attempt. If you want to eat it chilled, you can, but it's so delicious and easy right out of the blender that there's no reason to make things more difficult! Once you've mastered the base dessert, you can change it up a bit by adding different spices like cinnamon, vanilla powder, or even a pinch of cayenne for some heat.

Combine all the ingredients in a blender and blend until smooth. Scoop out and enjoy.

tropical coconut parfait

NUT-FREE · SOY-FREE · UNDER $10 · UNDER 30 MINUTES

SERVES 2 · PREP: 15 MINUTES

1 mango, peeled, pitted, and diced

1 cup diced pineapple

Juice of 1 lime

1 cup chopped fresh coconut meat, from 1 young Thai coconut

¼ cup coconut water

2 tablespoons pure maple syrup or raw honey

For a taste of the tropics, this quick, fruity parfait is perfect. It's not too sweet, which means you could also have it for a special occasion breakfast if you like. In that case, give it a bit more staying power by topping it with some homemade raw granola (see page 58). Be sure to dice the mango and pineapple evenly to give this dish an even more beautiful visual appeal. I like to cheat with a little maple syrup on mine, but if you want to make it completely raw, use honey instead.

1. Combine the mango and pineapple in a bowl. Toss with the lime juice.

2. Combine the coconut meat, coconut water, and maple syrup in a blender. Blend until smooth, with a whipped-cream consistency.

3. In jars or glasses, layer the fruit, then the coconut cream, followed by another layer of fruit and another layer of coconut cream. Serve immediately.

honey-banana ice cream

NUT-FREE · SOY-FREE · UNDER $10 · UNDER 30 MINUTES

SERVES 1 · PREP: 5 MINUTES

1 banana, chopped
   and frozen

1 tablespoon raw honey

This super easy ice cream is made even simpler if you freeze the banana in advance. Ideally, this ice cream should be made in a food processor. If you're not using a food processor, be sure to chop the banana very finely ahead of time, and have some nut milk on hand in case you need to thin out the mixture a bit.

Combine the frozen banana and honey in a food processor or blender. Process until the banana is creamy and smooth, about 5 minutes. Serve immediately.

SUBSTITUTION: This is really just a base recipe; once you try it, you won't be able to stop imagining add-ins! A few of my favorites include a swirl of nut butter, a handful of crushed nuts, cacao nibs, a drizzle of honey, or even a few spices. Let your imagination be your guide! Keep frozen bananas in the freezer at all times. You never know when an ice cream craving might hit.

mixed berry crumble

SOY-FREE

SERVES 4 · PREP: 20 MINUTES · DEHYDRATING: 4 HOURS

1 cup raw buckwheat groats,
soaked for 2 hours
and drained

½ cup raw almonds, soaked
for 8 hours and drained

½ cup raw hazelnuts, soaked
for 8 hours and drained

½ cup raw unsweetened
shredded coconut

¼ cup raw cacao nibs

½ cup raw honey

2 tablespoons coconut oil

1 teaspoon ground
cinnamon

1 cup chopped fresh
strawberries

1 cup fresh raspberries

1 cup fresh blackberries

1 cup fresh blueberries

Juice of ½ lemon

Coconut sugar

In this dish, a nutty crumble mixture is scattered over fresh fruit, which is just lightly bruised to bring out its natural sweetness. It's sweet enough for a dessert, but it's not too sweet to serve as breakfast as well.

1. Turn your oven to its lowest setting; if you have an oven thermometer, check to see that it doesn't go above 100 degrees. Line a baking sheet with parchment paper.

2. In a large bowl, stir together the groats, almonds, hazelnuts, shredded coconut, cacao nibs, honey, coconut oil, and cinnamon until well combined. Spread the mixture out on the lined baking sheet. Place the crumble in the oven and prop the door open so that it does not overheat. Dehydrate until the crumble sticks together in clumps, about 4 hours. Set aside.

3. In a bowl, toss the strawberries, raspberries, blackberries, and blueberries with the lemon juice. Mix with a wooden spoon until slightly muddled. Add a touch of coconut sugar as needed to sweeten the berries.

4. Transfer the berries to a serving dish or individual ramekins and top with the crumble. Serve.

SUBSTITUTION: Top the crumble with some homemade Honey-Banana Ice Cream (page 185).

raw apple pie

SOY-FREE · UNDER 30 MINUTES

SERVES 2 · PREP: 30 MINUTES

½ cup pecans, soaked for
   8 hours and drained

½ cup almonds, soaked for
   8 hours and drained

½ cup chopped dried
   pineapple

4 dates, pitted and chopped

1 cup raw cashews, soaked
   for 8 hours and drained

6 tablespoons raw
   apple juice

1 teaspoon raw honey

2 teaspoons ground
   cinnamon, divided

1 apple, cored and
   thinly sliced

Apple pie is an American classic, and this version has all the flavors you crave in a raw form. You will need large cookie cutters to build the individually sized tarts, or you can purchase professional pastry rings. Either way, these tarts are super impressive to serve.

1. Combine the pecans, almonds, pineapple, and dates in a blender or food processor. Blend or process until the ingredients stick together; the mixture does not need to be smooth, just sticky. Remove from the blender and press into a large round cookie cutter until you have an even crust. Rinse out the blender.

2. Combine the cashews, apple juice, honey, and 1 teaspoon of cinnamon in the blender and blend until you have a smooth cream. Spread the cream over the top of the crust.

3. Layer the apple slices over the top of the cream and sprinkle with the remaining 1 teaspoon of cinnamon. Serve.

raw pumpkin pie

SOY-FREE

SERVES 1 · PREP: 30 MINUTES · CHILLING: OVERNIGHT

FOR THE CRUST

½ cup hazelnuts, soaked for
8 hours and drained

¾ cup pecans, soaked for
8 hours and drained

½ cup dates, chopped

FOR THE FILLING

½ cup raw cashews, soaked
for 8 hours and drained

½ cup cubed pumpkin

2 tablespoons chia seeds

3 tablespoons unsweetened
hazelnut milk,
homemade (see page 79)
or store-bought

1 tablespoon raw honey

1 teaspoon ground
cinnamon

½ teaspoon ground cloves

½ teaspoon ground ginger

Freshly grated nutmeg

This raw pumpkin pie uses chia seeds to hold together the custard and is built in a large cookie cutter or small professional pastry ring. You'll need to chill the pie before serving to get the custard to hold, but it's worth the wait—the flavor of the pumpkin pie spices really comes through in this dish.

TO MAKE THE CRUST

Combine the hazelnuts, pecans, and dates in a blender or food processor. Blend or process until the ingredients stick together; the mixture does not need to be smooth, just sticky. Remove from the blender and press into a large round cookie cutter until you have an even crust. Press the crust up the sides of the cookie cutter to form a shell to hold the pumpkin cream inside. Rinse out the blender.

TO MAKE THE FILLING

Combine the ingredients for the filling in the blender and blend until you have a smooth cream. Spread the cream over the top of the crust, leaving the cookie cutter in place as a mold. Chill the pumpkin pie overnight so that the chia pumpkin filling can set. Remove the cookie cutter and serve.

raw banoffee pie

SOY-FREE

SERVES 2 · PREP: 1 HOUR

½ cup chopped fresh
coconut meat, from
1 young Thai coconut

1 tablespoon coconut oil

1 tablespoon coconut sugar

½ cup pecans, soaked for
8 hours and drained

½ cup almonds, soaked for
8 hours and drained

½ cup chopped dried
pineapple

1 cup chopped
dates, divided

¼ cup unsweetened cashew
milk, homemade (see
page 79) or store-bought

1 banana, thinly sliced

Think you can't have this classic dessert on raw? Think again. The nutty crust holds a date-sweetened "toffee" layer, and fresh banana and coconut whipped cream are the icing on this cake. You'll need to build these pies in large round cookie cutters or professional pastry rings in order to get everything to hold together beautifully.

1. Combine the coconut meat, coconut oil, and coconut sugar in a blender and blend until smooth, with a whipped-cream consistency. Transfer to a container and freeze for 30 minutes. Rinse out the blender.

2. Combine the pecans, almonds, pineapple, and ½ cup of dates in the blender or a food processor. Blend or process until the ingredients stick together; the mixture does not need to be smooth, just sticky. Remove from the blender and press into a large round cookie cutter until you have an even crust. Rinse out the blender.

3. Combine the cashew milk and the remaining ½ cup of dates in the blender and blend until you have a relatively smooth toffee. Spread the toffee over the top of the crust.

4. Layer the sliced bananas over the top of the cream. Top with the chilled coconut cream and serve.

raw carrot cake

SOY-FREE

SERVES 4 · PREP: 1 HOUR · CHILLING: OVERNIGHT

2 large carrots, peeled and grated, plus more for garnish

1 cup chopped dates

1 cup chopped dried pineapple

1 cup pecans, soaked for 8 hours and drained

½ cup raw buckwheat groats, soaked for 2 hours and drained

½ cup raw unsweetened coconut flakes

½ teaspoon ground cinnamon

½ teaspoon ground ginger

Freshly grated nutmeg

Pinch Himalayan salt

¼ cup raisins

2 cups cashews, soaked for 8 hours and drained

⅓ cup agave nectar

2 tablespoons coconut oil, plus more for greasing

1 tablespoon freshly squeezed orange juice

¼ cup unsweetened cashew milk, homemade (see page 79) or store-bought

Grated orange zest, for garnish

This moist carrot cake is relatively healthy and doesn't contain all that much sugar. It's also one of the only raw cakes you'll find that doesn't require the use of a dehydrator or oven, a plus for your electric bill. All you need is an overnight chill to get this cake to hold together. You'll be surprised at how sweet the result is.

1. Combine the carrots, dates, pineapple, pecans, groats, coconut flakes, cinnamon, ginger, nutmeg, and salt in a blender or food processor. Process until the mixture sticks together. Transfer to a bowl and fold in the raisins. Rinse out the blender.

2. Combine the cashews, agave, coconut oil, and orange juice in the blender and blend until creamy.

3. Grease four round cookie cutters with coconut oil. Press the carrot batter into them until it comes about halfway up. Spread a layer of cashew frosting over the top. Press a second layer of carrot batter on top of the frosting, pressing very carefully so as not to squish the frosting too much. Finish with a layer of frosting. Refrigerate overnight. Top with grated carrot and orange zest and serve.

raw shortbread sandwich cookies with raisin filling

SOY-FREE · UNDER $10

MAKES 12 · PREP: 15 MINUTES · CHILLING: 1 HOUR

1 cup almonds, soaked for 8 hours and drained

1 cup raw unsweetened coconut flakes

⅓ cup coconut oil

1 tablespoon agave nectar

Pinch Himalayan salt

1 cup raisins

¼ cup chopped dates

Grated zest and juice of 1 orange

Sometimes you just need to splurge, even on raw! These treats are quite rich, making them a true special occasion dessert. The cookies keep fairly well in the refrigerator or freezer; just don't spread the filling on until you're ready to eat them. You can store it separately in a jar in the refrigerator.

1. Line a baking sheet with parchment paper. Combine the almonds, coconut flakes, coconut oil, agave, and salt in a blender or food processor and blend until smooth. Press the shortbread mixture into a thin, even layer on the lined baking sheet and freeze for 1 hour. Rinse out the blender.

2. Meanwhile, combine the raisins, dates, orange zest, and orange juice in the blender or a food processor. Blend until the mixture sticks together; it doesn't need to be completely smooth.

3. Cut the chilled shortbread into even rectangles. Spread a spoonful of raisin filling on half the cookies, and top with the other half of the cookies. Serve.

cacao nib truffles

SOY-FREE

MAKES 24 TRUFFLES · PREP: 20 MINUTES · CHILLING: 1 HOUR

1½ cups sunflower seeds

1½ cups raw hazelnuts,
soaked for 8 hours
and drained

1½ cups dates, pitted

½ cup unsweetened
cocoa powder

1 tablespoon coconut oil

¼ teaspoon Himalayan salt

4 tablespoons cacao nibs

One of the secrets to finding satisfaction on a raw diet is seeking out the textures you crave. In these truffles, a combination of seeds and nuts makes the creamy ganache-like filling, sweetened with dates. The flavor of chocolate comes through in the raw cocoa powder and cacao nibs, making these little raw morsels a chocoholic's dream.

1. Combine the sunflower seeds and hazelnuts in a food processor and pulse until you achieve a sandy texture. Add the pitted dates and pulse until a paste forms. Add the cocoa powder, coconut oil, and salt and pulse until smooth.

2. Line a baking sheet with parchment paper. Use two spoons to portion out the mixture onto the lined baking sheet into 24 equal portions. Refrigerate for 30 minutes.

3. Remove from the refrigerator and roll the mixture into rounds between your palms. Roll each truffle in the cacao nibs and place on a plate or baking sheet. Refrigerate for an additional 30 minutes. Serve chilled.

SUBSTITUTION: Instead of cacao nibs, you can also roll your truffles in crushed nuts, more cocoa powder, raw unsweetened coconut flakes, or finely chopped goji berries.

raw almond joy bars

SOY-FREE · UNDER $10

MAKES 6 · PREP: 20 MINUTES · CHILLING: 30 MINUTES

1½ cups raw unsweetened coconut flakes

5 tablespoons agave nectar, divided

2 tablespoons coconut oil

Pinch Himalayan salt

⅓ cup melted cacao butter

⅓ cup unsweetened cocoa powder

12 raw almonds

I don't know about you, but I loved getting Almond Joy bars in my Halloween candy bag. This raw version is very close to the real thing. Leave out the almonds and you'll be left with raw Mounds bars, which, depending on who you ask, were even better.

1. Line a baking sheet with parchment paper. In a bowl, stir together the coconut flakes, 3 tablespoons of agave, the coconut oil, and salt. You may need to mix with your hands to get the mixture to stick together. Scoop into 6 equal portions and shape them into rectangles on the lined baking sheet. Refrigerate until fairly solid, about 30 minutes.

2. Meanwhile, in a bowl, whisk together the remaining 2 tablespoons of agave, melted cacao butter, and cocoa powder until smooth.

3. Dip each coconut bar into the coating and immediately top with two almonds. Refrigerate again until the chocolate sets, then serve.

RAW HUMMUS

CHAPTER 12

dips, dressings, sauces & spreads

shallot balsamic vinaigrette

MAKES ABOUT 1½ CUPS · PREP: 10 MINUTES

½ cup balsamic vinegar

1 cup extra-virgin olive oil

1 teaspoon Dijon mustard

1 shallot, halved

Himalayan salt

Freshly ground
   black pepper

If you have an immersion blender, this dressing is a snap. Just put all the ingredients in a jar, blend, close it up, and stick it in the refrigerator for later. This easy vinaigrette is perfect for any salad. Bear in mind that balsamic vinegar technically is not a raw ingredient; you can sub cider vinegar for balsamic vinegar, but add 1½ teaspoons agave nectar to get that added sweetness that balsamic brings to the party.

Combine all the ingredients in a blender and blend until smooth.

japanese orange-ginger salad dressing

NUT-FREE · UNDER $10 · UNDER 30 MINUTES

MAKES ABOUT 1 CUP · PREP: 10 MINUTES

2 carrots, peeled and grated

1 (1-inch) piece fresh
ginger, peeled

½ cup grapeseed oil

2 tablespoons tamari

2 tablespoons freshly
squeezed orange juice

2 tablespoons raw apple
cider vinegar

2 scallions, thinly sliced

This dressing was inspired by the orange-ginger dressing you frequently get at sushi restaurants. It's fantastic on a Japanese-inspired Buddha bowl, but it's also delicious on a simple bed of greens. You don't have to blend the dressing if you don't mind the texture of grated carrots; it can be delicious this way when tossed with thinly sliced or julienned vegetables.

Combine the carrots, ginger, grapeseed oil, tamari, orange juice, and cider vinegar in a blender and blend until smooth. Stir in the sliced scallions.

tahini salad dressing

MAKES ABOUT ½ CUP · PREP: 10 MINUTES

½ cup raw tahini
Juice of ½ lime
Juice of ¼ orange
1 tablespoon tamari
1 garlic clove, halved

Salad dressings can get a bit boring, particularly when you're always opting for vinaigrettes. This tahini salad dressing is a great alternative with tons of flavor. It has a bit of sweetness and acidity, but most of all it has a creaminess you wouldn't ever expect you could get from a dairy-free dressing. This dressing in particular is great on a kale salad with red onion and orange segments.

Combine all the ingredients in a blender and blend until smooth.

raw caesar dressing

UNDER 30 MINUTES

MAKES ABOUT 1 CUP · PREP: 10 MINUTES

¼ cup raw cashews, soaked
for 8 hours and drained

¼ cup raw hemp hearts,
soaked for 8 hours
and drained

¼ cup water

2 tablespoons extra-virgin
olive oil

1 tablespoon freshly
squeezed lemon juice

1 tablespoon
nutritional yeast

1½ teaspoons
Dijon mustard

1½ teaspoons tamari

1 garlic clove, halved

Freshly ground
black pepper

Caesar salad seems as though it would be anything but raw—eggs, cheese, anchovies, croutons—but with a bit of creativity, and this dressing, you can easily make a raw Caesar. My favorite raw Caesar recipe combines traditional romaine with kale, which has far more nutrients than the water-dense lettuce. You can also add your favorite sprouted legume for a bit more texture and protein.

Combine all the ingredients in a blender and blend until smooth.

raw ranch dressing

UNDER 30 MINUTES

MAKES ABOUT 1 CUP · PREP: 10 MINUTES

1 cup raw cashews, soaked
   for 8 hours and drained

2 garlic cloves, halved

1 shallot, halved

½ cup water

⅓ cup extra-virgin olive oil

¼ cup raw apple
   cider vinegar

3 tablespoons freshly
   squeezed lemon juice

1 teaspoon agave nectar

1 teaspoon tamari

1 teaspoon nutritional yeast

¼ cup chopped fresh
   parsley, dill, and/
   or chives

Ranch dressing is easy to replicate with a simple cashew base; all you need are a bunch of fresh herbs and the zing from nutritional yeast and lemon juice. The resulting dressing is awesome for dipping crudités or for pouring over your favorite salad recipe.

Combine the cashews, garlic, shallot, water, olive oil, cider vinegar, lemon juice, agave, tamari, and nutritional yeast in a blender and blend until smooth. Stir in the herbs and use immediately.

curry coconut sauce

NUT-FREE · SOY-FREE · UNDER 30 MINUTES

MAKES ABOUT 2 CUPS · PREP: 10 MINUTES

Water and chopped flesh
from 1 young
Thai coconut

1 red bell pepper, seeded
and roughly chopped

1 garlic clove, halved

1 scallion, white and light
green parts roughly
chopped, dark green
parts thinly sliced

½ Thai chile, seeded and
roughly chopped

1 (½-inch) piece fresh
ginger, peeled

1 teaspoon ground turmeric

1 teaspoon ground
coriander

1 teaspoon ground cumin

1 teaspoon cayenne pepper

Imagine your favorite Buddha bowl topped with a luxurious, creamy curry sauce. That's exactly what this offers. This sauce has a great orange color thanks to the red bell pepper and turmeric. You can vary the spices in the sauce according to your own tastes, particularly when it comes to the Thai chile—these peppers may be small, but they pack a huge heat!

Combine all the ingredients except for the dark green parts of the scallion in a blender and blend until smooth. Pour the sauce into a bowl and top with the dark green scallions.

habanero hot sauce

NUT-FREE · SOY-FREE · UNDER $10 · UNDER 30 MINUTES

MAKES ABOUT 1 CUP · PREP: 10 MINUTES

5 jalapeños, seeded and
   roughly chopped

5 red banana chiles, seeded
   and roughly chopped

5 habaneros, seeded and
   roughly chopped

4 garlic cloves, halved

1 cup raw apple
   cider vinegar

Juice of 1 lime

1 tablespoon agave nectar

If you like things spicy, this is the sauce for you! A little bit sweet, a little bit vinegary, and very, very spicy, this hot sauce is perfect for drizzling over your favorite dishes that need a bit of punch. Because every pepper is different, the heat in this sauce may vary. Taste your peppers before blending to get an idea of how hot the sauce will be, and feel free to remove the ribs and seeds of the peppers if you want lots of flavor but a bit less heat.

Combine all the ingredients in a blender and blend until smooth. Pour the sauce into a jar and store in the refrigerator.

PREP TIP: The oils in hot peppers like jalapeños and habaneros can actually burn your skin. Use gloves when handling, and be sure to wash all your tools immediately after preparing the sauce to avoid cross-contamination.

raw tomato sauce

NUT-FREE · SOY-FREE · UNDER $10 · UNDER 30 MINUTES

MAKES ABOUT 1 CUP · PREP: 10 MINUTES

2 beefsteak or other meaty
    tomatoes, chopped

4 sun-dried
    tomatoes, chopped

1 garlic clove, halved

1 tablespoon extra-virgin
    olive oil

Himalayan salt

Freshly ground
    black pepper

5 basil leaves, cut into
    chiffonade (see Prep Tip,
    page 96)

This tomato sauce is a great all-purpose sauce for your favorite cauliflower rice and zucchini noodle dishes. Be sure that you pick only the meatiest, juiciest tomatoes, as this way they'll be adding flavor, not water, to the sauce. No tomatoes—even prepared—should be kept in the refrigerator, as they lose their texture and flavor quickly, so make this sauce with room-temperature tomatoes just before you want to use it.

1. Combine the fresh and sun-dried tomatoes in a blender and blend until smooth. Add the garlic and olive oil and continue to blend. Season with salt and pepper.

2. Pour the sauce into a bowl. Stir in the basil and serve.

raw fermented ketchup

NUT-FREE · SOY-FREE · UNDER $10

MAKES ABOUT 1 CUP · PREP: 10 MINUTES · FERMENTING: AT LEAST 2 DAYS

1½ cups chopped meaty
    tomatoes

6 tablespoons sauerkraut
    brine, divided

¼ cup raw apple
    cider vinegar

5 tablespoons raw honey

Himalayan salt

Ketchup on raw? Yes, you can! This fermented ketchup recipe is full of good bacteria, making it a choice you can feel good about. The texture of this raw ketchup won't be exactly the same as what you would expect with a store-bought ketchup, but the rich tomato flavor and the zing of the vinegar will be present for sure.

In a blender, combine the tomatoes, 2 tablespoons of sauerkraut brine, cider vinegar, and honey, and season with salt. Blend until smooth. Transfer to a jar and cover with the remaining 4 tablespoons of brine, then cover with a cloth secured with a rubber band to the mouth of the jar. Ferment for 2 to 3 days at room temperature. When your ketchup has reached the desired consistency, transfer to the refrigerator.

raw cranberry sauce

NUT-FREE · SOY-FREE · UNDER $10 · UNDER 30 MINUTES

MAKES ABOUT 3 CUPS · PREP: 10 MINUTES

1 (10-ounce) bag
    cranberries

Grated zest and juice of
    1 orange

2 tablespoons raw honey

2 tablespoons agave nectar

1 pickled (or fresh) jalapeño,
    seeded and minced

This cranberry relish is a little bit sweet and a little bit spicy, perfect for putting atop a fall-inspired Buddha bowl with winter squash. You may have to adjust the sweetener in this recipe, depending on your cranberries. When cranberries are too acidic, they can be nearly acrid, so taste and adjust as needed.

Combine all the ingredients in a blender and pulse, keeping the mixture chunky and adding water as needed to thin. The cranberries should be broken up but not reduced to a purée.

pico de gallo

MAKES ABOUT 2 CUPS · PREP: 10 MINUTES

4 tomatoes, finely diced

1 white onion, finely diced

1 bunch cilantro, chopped

2 jalapeños, seeded
   and minced

Juice of 1 lime

Himalayan salt

This fresh tomato salsa gets its name from the "rooster's beak," which is a reference to the spice factor! The key to a perfect pico de gallo is chopping everything into a very fine dice. This salsa gets better with time, so feel free to make it a bit in advance and leave it on the counter to marinate before serving.

Toss together all the ingredients in a bowl.

berry coulis

NUT-FREE · SOY-FREE · UNDER 30 MINUTES

MAKES ABOUT 1 CUP · PREP: 10 MINUTES

½ cup quartered fresh
   strawberries
½ cup fresh raspberries
½ cup fresh blackberries
½ cup fresh blueberries
Juice of ½ orange

This berry coulis is perfect as a topping for your favorite raw ice cream or chia pudding recipe. Try not to make coulis too far in advance, as it will quickly lose its freshness. This recipe is also the ideal way to use up any bruised berries that you might find in your containers.

Combine all the ingredients in a blender and pulse until puréed but not entirely smooth.

PREP TIP: I like my coulis to have a chunkier texture so I still get the sensation of berries when I eat it, but you could also blend it until smooth or even run the finished purée through a fine-mesh strainer to make a syrup.

spicy tahini sauce

MAKES ABOUT 1 CUP · PREP: 10 MINUTES

½ cup raw tahini

Juice of ½ lemon

1 jalapeño, seeded

1 Thai chile, seeded

1 garlic clove, halved

1 tablespoon agave nectar

Raw tahini is a powerful superfood, with one of the highest oil contents of any seed, making it an important addition to calorie-poor raw vegan diets. The oils in tahini are mostly oleic and linoleic acids, both of which are healthy fats that are essential in a raw food diet. This sauce is very versatile and lovely on a salad with a bit of sweetness, like some citrus segments, to balance the spice in the sauce.

1. In a bowl, whisk together the tahini, lemon juice, and water as needed until you have a dippable texture.

2. Combine the jalapeño, chile, garlic, and agave in a blender and blend until smooth.

3. Carefully pour a swirl of the chile mixture over the top of the tahini. Serve.

muhammara

MAKES ABOUT 2 CUPS · PREP: 10 MINUTES

1 cup walnuts, soaked for 8
    hours and drained

¼ cup raw pine nuts

3 red bell peppers, seeded
    and chopped

4 sun-dried
    tomatoes, minced

1 garlic clove, minced

⅓ cup extra-virgin olive oil

Juice of ½ lemon

½ teaspoon ground sumac

½ teaspoon ground cumin

½ teaspoon cayenne pepper

This Middle Eastern sauce may not be as well known as hummus or baba ghanouj, but it's just as delicious and lends itself perfectly to a raw food version. With its combination of earthy walnuts and sweet bell peppers, this dip is perfect for Buddha bowls or as an accompaniment to Raw Falafel (page 141).

Combine all the ingredients in a blender and blend until relatively smooth; you can serve the dip slightly chunky as well, according to your personal preference. If you find that the mixture is too thick, add extra olive oil or a bit of water to help the blender blades turn.

perfect guacamole

NUT-FREE · SOY-FREE · UNDER $10 · UNDER 30 MINUTES

MAKES ABOUT 2 CUPS · PREP: 10 MINUTES

1 tomato, finely chopped

1 red onion, finely chopped

Himalayan salt

2 avocados, halved
    and pitted

Juice of 1 lime

Chopped fresh cilantro,
    for garnish

Guacamole is a naturally raw dish that everyone can agree on. Instead of chips, use crudités as dippers or serve a spoonful on top of any Mexican-inspired raw dish. This version of guacamole is very chunky, almost more salad than dip, but feel free to mash the avocado a bit more if you like.

1. In a bowl, combine the tomato and red onion, and season with salt. Set aside.

2. Cut a very fine score into the flesh of each avocado half, cutting all the way to the skin. Use a spoon to scoop the avocado chunks into another bowl and mash very lightly. You should have a little bit of mash, but mostly chunks. Season with lime juice and mix to combine.

3. Start spooning in the tomato and onion mixture, bit by bit, stirring with each addition. When you have enough tomato and onion for your liking, season the guacamole with salt, garnish with cilantro, and serve.

raw hummus with za'atar and pomegranate

NUT-FREE · SOY-FREE · UNDER 30 MINUTES

MAKES ABOUT 1 CUP · PREP: 10 MINUTES

2 cups sprouted chickpeas
   (see page 34)

2 tablespoons raw tahini

2 tablespoons extra-
   virgin olive oil, plus
   1 tablespoon for drizzling

2 garlic cloves, halved

Juice of 1 lemon

Pinch Himalayan salt

1 tablespoon za'atar
   seasoning blend

Arils from 1 pomegranate

Raw chickpeas are some of the most nutrient-dense legumes when sprouted. They also make a delicious hummus. This one likely won't come out as creamy as standard hummus unless you have a high-speed blender, but that doesn't make it any less delicious. The pomegranate arils sprinkled over the top not only add beautiful color, but they contribute a healthy dose of antioxidants as well.

1. Combine the chickpeas, tahini, 2 tablespoons of olive oil, garlic, lemon juice, and salt in a blender. Blend until smooth, drizzling in a bit of water as you blend to reach the right consistency.

2. Transfer the hummus to a bowl. Drizzle with the remaining 1 tablespoon of olive oil, then sprinkle on the za'atar and the pomegranate arils. Serve.

DIY HACK: If you can't find za'atar seasoning blend in the store, you can make your own. Combine equal parts minced fresh thyme, raw sesame seeds, and ground sumac, and season with a pinch of Himalayan salt.

raw broccoli hummus

SOY-FREE · UNDER $10 · UNDER 30 MINUTES

SERVES 4 · PREP: 10 MINUTES

1 head broccoli, cut into bite-size pieces

¼ cup raw cashews, soaked for 8 hours and drained

1 zucchini, cut into pieces

1 garlic clove, halved

⅓ cup raw tahini

2 tablespoons freshly squeezed lemon juice

¼ cup extra-virgin olive oil

Himalayan salt

Raw black sesame seeds, for garnish

Broccoli is one of the best vegetable sources of calcium, though dairy proponents would have you think otherwise. Because dark leafy greens like kale and spinach also contain oxalates, which bind to calcium and make it harder to absorb, their high calcium content is often for naught. But broccoli's 70 milligrams of calcium per cup is absorbed up to 60 percent, making it a great veggie source of the mineral.

1. Combine the broccoli and cashews in a blender or food processor and blitz until a chunky paste forms. Add the zucchini, garlic, tahini, and lemon juice and continue blending, scraping down the sides as needed, until the mixture starts to come together. Drizzle in the olive oil while the blender is turning until it is fully incorporated and the hummus is smooth.

2. Taste the hummus and season with salt as needed. Transfer the hummus to a serving bowl and garnish with the raw sesame seeds.

creamy avocado dip

NUT-FREE · SOY-FREE · UNDER $10 · UNDER 30 MINUTES

MAKES ABOUT 1 CUP · PREP: 10 MINUTES

1 avocado, peeled, pitted,
    and cubed

1 shallot, halved

¼ cup fresh parsley leaves

Juice of ½ lemon

1 teaspoon ground cumin

This simple, creamy dip is super easy to make and full of flavor. It's the ideal snack with a pile of raw veggies. If you don't feel like pulling out the blender just to make this dip, you can also crush the ingredients with a fork for a chunkier dip, closer in texture to guacamole.

Combine all the ingredients in a blender and blend until creamy.

hemp heart and cashew "cheese" dip

SOY-FREE · UNDER 30 MINUTES

MAKES ABOUT 1½ CUPS · PREP: 10 MINUTES

½ cup hemp hearts, soaked
for 8 hours and drained

½ cup raw cashews, soaked
for 8 hours and drained

1 red bell pepper, seeded
and roughly chopped

¼ cup nutritional yeast

4 to 5 tablespoons water

2 tablespoons extra-virgin
olive oil

2 tablespoons freshly
squeezed lemon juice

Himalayan salt

Freshly ground
black pepper

Hemp hearts are a fantastic superfood containing not only a great balance of omega fatty acids, but also gamma linolenic acid and a number of important vitamins and minerals. Their earthy flavor lends a touch of pungency to this cheesy dip, which I love.

Combine all the ingredients in a blender and blend until smooth.

kale pesto

SOY-FREE · UNDER $10 · UNDER 30 MINUTES

MAKES ABOUT 1 CUP · PREP: 10 MINUTES

¼ cup raw pine nuts

1 garlic clove, halved

1 tablespoon
nutritional yeast

1 cup basil leaves

1 cup baby kale

½ cup extra-virgin olive oil

Himalayan salt

Freshly ground
black pepper

This kale pesto has an earthier flavor than many pure basil pestos. I like the umami flavor of the kale, which adds a bit more of the "cheesiness" that a traditional pesto has. It's also much richer in antioxidants and flavonoids than basil alone.

Combine the pine nuts, garlic, and nutritional yeast in a blender and pulse a few times to break up the garlic clove and pine nuts. Add the basil leaves and kale and a drizzle of the olive oil. Blend on low speed, slowly drizzling in the remaining olive oil, until the pesto is smooth. Do not overblend, or you risk oxidizing the basil. Season the pesto with salt and pepper.

SUBSTITUTION: You can swap the kale for any other leafy green, like spinach or arugula, for a different flavor.

THE DIRTY DOZEN
& THE CLEAN FIFTEEN

A nonprofit and environmental watchdog organization called the Environmental Working Group (EWG) looks at data supplied by the US Department of Agriculture (USDA) and the Food and Drug Administration (FDA) about pesticide residues. Each year it compiles a list of the lowest and highest pesticide loads found in commercial crops. You can use these lists to decide which fruits and vegetables to buy organic to minimize your exposure to pesticides and which produce is considered safe enough to buy conventionally. This does not mean they are pesticide-free, though, so wash these fruits and vegetables thoroughly.

These lists change every year, so make sure you look up the most recent one before you fill your shopping cart. You'll find the most recent lists as well as a guide to pesticides in produce at EWG.org/FoodNews.

DIRTY DOZEN

Apples	Strawberries
Celery	Sweet bell peppers
Cherry tomatoes	*In addition to the dirty dozen, the EWG added two produce contaminated with highly toxic organophosphate insecticides:*
Cucumbers	
Grapes	
Nectarines (imported)	
Peaches	Kale/Collard greens
Potatoes	Hot peppers
Snap peas (imported)	
Spinach	

CLEAN FIFTEEN

Asparagus	Kiwis
Avocados	Mangos
Cabbage	Onions
Cantaloupes (domestic)	Papayas
Cauliflower	Pineapples
Eggplants	Sweet corn
Grapefruits	Sweet peas (frozen)
	Sweet potatoes

MEASUREMENT CONVERSION TABLES

VOLUME EQUIVALENTS (LIQUID)

US STANDARD	US STANDARD (OUNCES)	METRIC (APPROXIMATE)
2 tablespoons	1 fl. oz.	30 mL
¼ cup	2 fl. oz.	60 mL
½ cup	4 fl. oz.	120 mL
1 cup	8 fl. oz.	240 mL
1½ cups	12 fl. oz.	355 mL
2 cups or 1 pint	16 fl. oz.	475 mL
4 cups or 1 quart	32 fl. oz.	1 L
1 gallon	128 fl. oz.	4 L

OVEN TEMPERATURES

FAHRENHEIT (F)	CELSIUS (C) (APPROXIMATE)
250°F	120°C
300°F	150°C
325°F	165°C
350°F	180°C
375°F	190°C
400°F	200°C
425°F	220°C
450°F	230°C

VOLUME EQUIVALENTS (DRY)

US STANDARD	METRIC (APPROXIMATE)
⅛ teaspoon	0.5 mL
¼ teaspoon	1 mL
½ teaspoon	2 mL
¾ teaspoon	4 mL
1 teaspoon	5 mL
1 tablespoon	15 mL

WEIGHT EQUIVALENTS

US STANDARD	METRIC (APPROXIMATE)
½ ounce	15 g
1 ounce	30 g
2 ounces	60 g
4 ounces	115 g
8 ounces	225 g
12 ounces	340 g

REFERENCES

Boutenko, Victoria. "Raw Family." Accessed December 7, 2015. www.rawfamily.com.

Carillo-Bucaram, Kristina. "Fully Raw." Accessed December 7, 2015. www.fullyraw.com.

Haupt, Angela. "Raw Food Diet." *U.S. News and World Report*. Accessed December 7, 2015. health.usnews.com/best-diet/raw-food-diet.

Helene, Zoe, and Chris Kilham. "Medicine Hunter." Accessed December 7, 2015. www.medicinehunter.com.

Love, Elaina. "Elaina Love's Blog." Accessed December 7, 2015. www.elainalove.com.

"Naturally Savvy." Accessed December 7, 2015. www.naturallysavvy.com.

Patenaude, Frederic. "Frederic Patenaude." Accessed December 7, 2015. www.fredericpatenaude.com.

Powers, Susan. "Rawmazing." Accessed December 7, 2015. www.rawmazing.com.

"Raw Food Recipes." Accessed December 7, 2015. www.rawfoodrecipes.com.

Sarno, Chad. "Chad Sarno." Accessed December 7, 2015. www.rawchef.com.

Stevens, Esme. "The Best of Raw Food." Accessed December 7, 2015. www.thebestofrawfood.com.

RECIPE INDEX

INDEX